W9-AVK-595

HITLER
AND THE
OCCULT

HITLER
AND THE
OCCULT

KEN ANDERSON

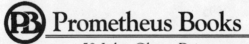

Prometheus Books

59 John Glenn Drive
Amherst, NewYork 14228-2197

Published 1995 by Prometheus Books

99 98 97 96 95   5 4 3 2 1

Library of Congress Cataloging-in-Publication Data

Anderson, Ken.
    Hitler and the occult / Ken Anderson.
        p.   cm.
    Includes bibliographical references and index.
    ISBN 0-87975-973-9
    1. Hitler, Adolf, 1889–1945. 2. National socialism and occultism.
3. Occultism—Germany. I. Title.
DD247.H5A8154   1995
943.086′092—dc20   95-3701
                                                      CIP

Printed in the United States of America on acid-free paper.

To Chloe who loved life

Contents

Part Two: Hitler and the Cosmos   173

Acknowledgments

I am deeply grateful to Martin Cochrane who organized my research efforts with much patience and to Steven L. Mitchell, the Editor-in-Chief of Prometheus Books, and Assistant Editor Mary A. Read for their commitment to excellence and accuracy; their professionalism, insightfulness, and constructive suggestions.

For permission to use the photographs in this book I would like to thank Mirror Australian Telegraph Publications photo library and Ms. Shirley Griffin. I have made every effort to contact the holder of the copyright for each picture. In several cases these sources have been untraceable for which I offer my apologies.

Introduction

Shortly before the start of World War II Adolf Hitler was talking persistently in terms of a German Master Race that would rule over a "Thousand-year Reich."

The nineteenth-century philosopher Friedrich Nietzsche had prophesied the evolution of such a race. His contemporary, the composer Richard Wagner whose German folkloric operas so enraptured Hitler, designated the Germans as the people who would comprise this super race (although Nietzsche disagreed), saying its advent was imminent.[1]

As though to prove his belief in Wagner's prophecy, Hitler went to war. Driven by what appeared to be an uncanny instinct and unwavering certainty, the Nazi leader, who had ignored the advice of his generals about starting and pursuing the war, personally gave the orders for its conduct. As a consequence he forced astonishing victory after victory throughout 1939–40.

The western European nations having been conquered or subjugated, he turned on his temporary ally Russia, and with further victories in the East he set about creating a slave nation that would do the bidding of its Master Race rulers.

By mid-1942 Hitler had reached the height of his hegemony: sole ruler of an immense land mass, from the Arctic circle to the desert sands of Africa, from the western Atlantic shores of

France to the Caspian Sea. Above this empire flew the Nazi's talisman of power, the swastika.

But even as he gloated the gods appeared to become sated by his excesses and turned on their prodigal in a way that would have done a Wagnerian plot proud. Russia halted the German army, then began winning back its lost lands. The major bastion of democracy, the United States, came to the rescue of Western civilization. In North Africa, the Rommel Korps was defeated and the Allies turned their growing power to the recovery of Europe. Sicily was invaded, then Italy itself. In the greatest amphibious operation in history, in June 1944 an Allied armada successfully landed an overwhelming force on the heavily fortified coast of France. In the east Soviet forces fought their way across Germany to Berlin, to the bunker whose thick concrete walls had become the shrunken boundaries of that great empire of a few short years before.

Hitler's "Thousand-year Reich" ended with his suicide in the bunker on 30 April 1945. The illusion that the Germans were a Master Race over all others died with Hitler. But by then millions had perished in the total war he had unleashed. They included both combatants and civilians—men, women, and children.

Millions more were systematically enslaved, deported, tortured, and slaughtered. Behind this subjugation of an entire race and others who appeared to oppose the regime—or were deemed unfit to serve it—were tens of thousands of "ordinary" people who had been convinced by the Hitler myth to debase and destroy their fellow humans in a manner and with a ferocity and scale never before seen in history. These controllers of Hitler's living hell, the mass murderers, executioners, and guards were not made up of the dregs of humanity. There were many professionals among them, including doctors who carried out appalling experiments, planners who organized the deportation to the death camps, engineers who designed and built the ovens and gas chambers, and members of the legal system.

If there is one thing that sets the Hitler regime apart from the Stalin regime in which millions also died, it is the Holocaust.

The equally brutal Stalinist system used extermination as a means to an end, the Nazis used extermination as an end in itself.

For all intents and purposes Hitler had been transfixed through the compulsion of his adoration for Wagner to stage an obscene version of one of the composer's works using the world as his stage. His own stupendous version of *Gottedammerung* (the twilight of the gods) saw fire, blood, and slaughter (extermination) without mercy and without any sense of human perspective. As chancellor, Hitler had averred that the seeds of Nazism had been sown at the first *Rienzi* he had attended as a teenager in his home town of Linz. In this Wagner work the hero unifies a divided people.[2] Hitler had also said that to understand national socialism Germany must first know Wagner.[3]

As the false Wagnerian climax faded the world awoke to a new dawn. It was a time for hope and also a time of questions. How could one man alone have created this monstrous regime which he alone ran until the very last moment of his life? From where had he come? Where did he draw his power; his Nietzschean will; his certainty of action; his ability to *mesmerize* people, masses, and nations? What primitive and dark core had he struck in those "normal" people who had operated the death camps where the destruction of the European Jewish race and modern civilization had come so close to being a reality? Was he a product of some occultic force? As we shall see, Hitler alluded to some ill-defined force directing him, which he called Providence.

And what of the lesser Nazis, his close disciples who did his bidding? They, too, were brutal and without mercy. Stripped to their essence their crimes were outlined at the Nuremberg war crimes tribunal as inhuman acts against the civilian population in occupied territories; persecution of people for political, racial, and religious reasons; and contravention of the law of war and the conventions of war. Were they a result of mental aberrations? Or were their actions affected by the occult such as the black magic rites allegedly indulged in by SS leader Heinrich Himmler; the arcane practices and beliefs that so intrigued and compelled Hitler's deputy Rudolf Hess; or Propaganda Minister Joseph

Goebbels's beliefs in fate, destiny, and reincarnation? Goebbels claimed that in every one of Hitler's previous lives he, too, had been reborn along with Hitler.[4]

At this stage we should pause to consider the meaning of "occult." It is a broad term but in essence it means that which is beyond the bounds of ordinary knowledge. Magic rituals, for example, are generally considered occultic. The occult is the unknown, the mysterious. It is often found intermingled with folklore as a part of a national mythology which speaks of magic, potions and spells, ogres, superhuman heroes, and the like. Such stories inspired Wagner.

In a perverse way placing Hitler and the Nazi elite into the world of mystery brings a certain comfort to many who find it difficult even today to acknowledge the Hitler hegemony as a chapter in the history of humanity.

We cannot argue against the proposition by using personal testimony because those who would have provided it—Hitler, Himmler, Goebbels, and the like—did not survive. Hess spent the post-war years until he died as a political prisoner, condemned to silence for his intriguing role in the war (see chapter 20).

Stories claiming Hitler was under the influence of some occultic force or forces have been around since the 1920s, that is, early in the days of the Nazi era. Following the war these claims gathered strength with the publication of more books that appear to detail occultic links with Hitler and the Nazis. Today the claims are accepted in some quarters as an integral, even an explanatory part, of the story of Hitler.

The life of Hitler from his birth in an Austrian village on 20 April 1889 is examined in detail in the chapters of this book. The point needs to be made here that he came to adulthood in the dying days of the Austro-Hungarian empire and the reawakening of the Pan-German movement in Austria. While the old empire faded, Germany across the border was growing in stature. By World War I it was one of the most advanced industrial nations in Europe. It presented a beacon to draw the admiration of idealistic German-speaking peoples such as Hitler.

However, there was a more sinister attraction which he would also have had difficulty ignoring: "Over this hard-working country seemingly so sure of its future, with rapidly growing metropolises and industrial areas, there arched a peculiarly romantic sky whose darkness was populated by mythic figures, antiquated giants, and ancient deities. . . . A good deal of professional obscurantinism and Teutonic folklorism was involved."[5]

Politically Hitler was imbued early with the ideals of German nationalism and *Anschluss,* the ancient German dream of unification. He was also, as we shall see, a voracious reader of an indiscriminate variety of subjects which may have generated incipient thoughts of his own importance and his early belief in his glorious destiny.

Hitler was inspired by both the music and the philosophy of Wagner. Wagner was anti-Semitic. He believed the virtues of the Teuton tribes had atrophied with the coming of the industrial revolution; that courage and will had been poisoned or emasculated by capitalism and race pollution; that the Jews were responsible for the enervation and enslavement of the German spirit; and that a new Siegfried must arise to lead the Germans to an awareness of their greatness.*

A strong undercurrent of anti-Semitic strains ran in the Viennese society in which Hitler spent his late teenage and early adult years. It would have taken a far more singular-minded lad, seeking but largely failing to make a place for himself, not to have been influenced by those strains, although his personal experiences with Jews had been cordial.

When World War I erupted in 1914, Hitler rushed to enlist

---

*Siegfried, a legendary Germanic hero, is the main character in Wagner's *Ring* cycle, who is deceived and speared in the back by his enemies as the opera reaches its climax. The war had acted as a catalyst for the movements of both political and social revolution in Europe. At its start there had been seventeen monarchies and three republics in Europe. At war's end the numbers were equal; the trend was obvious and frightening to many. The German kaiser had been among the monarchs toppled. Czarist Russia was swept away in the Communist revolution whose tentacles were spreading to Germany.

in the German army. He fought well and with the conviction that Germans as the superior race must win. He won the Iron Cross, First Class. But Germany lost to the military superiority of the Allies. It was a blow which he and millions of other Germans could not accept. Many claimed they had not been beaten on the field of battle but stabbed in the back—like Siegfried—the treacherous person in this case being their own leaders who had capitulated.

Many of those Germans who would not acknowledge the reality created by the war organized into a fantastic swarm of racist-nationalist parties, clubs, and free corps. Some attracted the petty bourgeois elements, others the peasants, yet others the working class.[6] These were generally conservative groups, opposed to the changing face of Europe. They saw the Jew as a threat to their largely imagined idyllic past with its stability and values. The Jew was behind communism; he was the greedy face of capitalism; he was the voice urging the suppression of the Teutonic traditions.

One of these organizations was the German Workers party. Its origins were not a result of a spontaneous action by members of the working class. Rather it had been founded by the Thule Society, largely made up in the immediate post-war period of members of the upper echelons of Bavarian society. "Thule" in folklore is the mythical north Atlantic island from which came the first members of Nordic civilization.

As we shall see in chapter 11, occult writers claim that some of these latter-day Thulists believed they were direct descendants of this early Northern race. Some members, it is alleged, practiced bizarre magic rituals. Hence a direct link between Hitler and the occultists is supposedly drawn. In September 1919 Hitler became a member of the Workers party. While still in the army he had been assigned to infiltrate the party. At a meeting he had demanded to speak when a member had argued for the annexation of Bavaria from Germany to Austria. The oratorical skills displayed in his strong opposition to the proposal led to the party leaders inviting him to join. Hitler was to write later of his decision to accept as the turning point in his life. There are suggestions he believed he had arrived at this point by predetermined destiny, the guiding hand of Providence. An objective examination would suggest he was affected more by chance than convergence.

On 16 October 1919, a month after his "spy" mission, Hitler addressed his first public meeting on the party's behalf. Hitler biographer Joachim Fest describes it:

> In a bitter stream of words, the dammed-up emotions, the lonely man's suffocated feelings of hatred and impotence burst out, like an explosion after the restriction and apathy of the years, hallucinatory images and accusations came pouring out; abandoning restraint, he talked until he was sweating and exhausted.
>
> Wildly acclaimed by his audience, Hitler had discovered that he could wield "the magic power of the spoken word."[7]

As news of his oratorical abilities spread, each meeting drew more followers. Hitler came to the attention of influential Bavarians who encouraged and backed him, finding funds from wealthy members of society and Russian emigrés afraid of the spread of Communism. Hamburg, the Bavarian capital, was one of the cities that had fallen to the Communists in the thwarted revolution of 1919. It was recovered in a bloody counterattack in which the Thule society supplied arms to the counterrevolutionaries. A number of Thulists had been captured and executed by the Reds.

Hitler soon took control of the party. In 1920 he changed its name to the National Socialists, which became abbreviated to the Nazis. As we have seen there were many such parties where beer drinking seemed to be one of the reasons for their gatherings. What then made Hitler's Nazis stand out and survive? Undoubtedly it was in large part due to the personality of Hitler himself.

He was articulating the passions and frustrations of party members—and a great many other Germans—in the voice of a working-class hero. He spoke for those who felt disenfranchised and alienated, and he did it brilliantly.

There were setbacks. A 1923 coup attempt by party members resulted in the jailing of Hitler and other Nazis. However, Hitler turned the incident into a plus with a stirring address to the judges in which he concluded, "I consider myself not a traitor, but a German who wanted the best for the German people." His words were greeted with applause from the crowded courtroom. The trial itself was front-page news in every German newspaper. By its end Hitler had become a national figure.[8]

Among the leaders of Bavarian society who had given Hitler and the Nazis protection were Munich Chief of Police Ernst Pohner, his political adviser Wilhelm Frick, and Bavarian Minister of Justice Franz Gurtner. All were allegedly Thulists and shared Hitler's nationalistic rightist views. Both Frick and Gurtner joined the party and were given ministries when Hitler became chancellor. Although Hitler was sentenced to five years, largely through the influence of these future Nazis he spent less than nine months in jail. He used the time to write his turgid autobiography *Mein Kampf* (My Struggle), which was to become the Nazi "bible."

At the helm once again, Hitler set about introducing some "color" into the grey blanket of German politics. He used bright red in banners and on posters—a direct steal from the parties of the Left. He sent disciplined paramilitary forces—old soldiers, new Nazis—through the streets on trucks and in parades. He organized torchlight processions and the strains of Wagner's music were heard at rallies.

He also took trouble over the introduction of some simple but effective symbols, including the raised arm, open-handed salute that was linked with the traditional German greeting "Heil," to become the alliterative "Heil, Hitler." He adopted the eagle, an ancient heraldic device, as the party's official symbol, and, of course, the swastika (see chapter 12). As public relations gimmicks they were highly successful in creating a fascination with the party and Hitler among a people used to a blander presentation of the political "product."

Hitler added another touch by growing his own version of the by-then celebrated moustache of Charlie Chaplin. Even today a black oblong is all that is needed to put many people in mind of both men. It was rumored in Germany that Hitler's seemingly bizarre action had been to cash in on Chaplin's popularity.[9] Harry

Geduld of Indiana University, professor of comparative literature, points out that the Nazis denounced Chaplin as a "Bolshevik Jew," so he finds Hitler's motivation in taking on the famous "trademark" of a man who exemplified all that he most abhorred a mystery.[10] However, Hitler was capable of borrowing from any source. He picked up his tactics and aims "from all the bushes along the road of life," writes Fest.[11]

The symbolism became a part of the Hitler myth. To bolster the myth further, Hitler set about redefining his past. In the beginning he had "nothing at all to back [him], nothing, no name, no fortune, no press, nothing at all, nothing whatsoever."[12]

Many of those who had known and worked with him in the early days were either silenced through execution or, if they were fortunate enough to escape death, through censorship or intimidation. An appropriate example is Lanz Von Liebenfels, a defrocked monk who was deeply involved in astrology and racism. The significance of their relationship is dealt with in chapter 2. In 1938 Hitler forbade this eccentric racist philosopher to publish.[13]

It is argued by some of the occultic writers we meet in these pages that by jailing or otherwise disposing of occultists as he did in many cases, Hitler not only hid his past connections with them but ensured that his was the only occultic force in power. Against that we have the fact Hitler never moved in any substantial way against the nation's greatest repository of occultic lore and influence—the church.

The Hitler myth rose to new heights under Joseph Goebbels, who became the Nazi propaganda chief. "The power of the myth derived precisely from the fact that it was a combination of genuine, popular belief and sophisticated manipulation," Bullock writes. "Hitler was both presented and seen by the party and by millions of Germans outside it as the embodiment of *Volksgemeinschaft* [national unity] standing above sectional interests; the architect of Germany's recovery, personally incorruptible. A fanatical defender of German honor and Germany's just rights against both internal and external enemies—yet a man of the people."[14]

Polls showed that from about the mid-1920s on Hitler enjoyed enormous popularity. Part of the reason may well have been the lack of well-defined policies and ideologies, allowing people to see in Hitler what they wanted to see.

Even so, it is worth remembering that the Nazis initially came to power not through some mysterious process or even a coup, but through the ballot box. At the 1930 elections the Nazis gained 107 seats in the Reichstag—mainly from the moderates—to become the second largest party in government. In 1933 the Nazis and their allies, the Nationalists, gained slightly more than half the seats. Hitler, who had been appointed chancellor by President von Hindenburg earlier that year at a time of political crisis, demanded and was given the right to rule by decree for four years to restore order.

Once the power was in his hands, he refused to relinquish it. His next steps were to gather the German people under one banner. United, the Master Race would fulfill its "historical destiny." In 1938 Austria was annexed, and then the German-speaking parts of Czechoslovakia. The race was one, *Anschluss* achieved.

At this stage Hitler had no need to believe in anything except himself or feel that he was under the control of any power but his own. He had hypnotized a people and gone on to do the same thing with much of the world. In the process he had dabbled in many ideas and philosophies. He had used and discarded people and organizations who had looked to him as the man who could work miracles, even making people believe they were on the point of living in an idyllic society of Teutonic order and values in which the lesser races would do their bidding. One of the few things that Hitler remained loyal to was the music of Wagner and the composer's prognostications on German mythology and the Jewish people.

Apart from providing a background for the rest of this book, the purpose of this introduction has been to show in as rational a way as possible a thread of the occult in the story of Hitler. It is a subtle, pervasive, troubling, even fascinating thread which for the sake of historical truth must be examined more closely than some of the proponents of the view that the occult was a major influence on Hitler are willing to do.

Notes

1. Gerald Suster, *The Occult Messiah* (New York: St. Martin's Press, 1981), p. 9.

2. Steven R. Cerf, Professor of German, Bowdoin College, in an article in *Opera News,* 31 March 1990, p. 18.

3. Suster, *The Occult Messiah,* p. 9.

4. Francis King, *Satan and Swastika,* quoted in Michael FitzGerald, *Stormtroopers of Satan* (London: Robert Hale, 1990), p. 110.

5. Joachim C. Fest, *Hitler* (Hammondsworth, Middlesex, U.K.: Pelican Books, 1977), p. 143.

6. Ibid., pp. 133–34.

7. Joachim C. Fest, *The Face of the Third Reich,* quoted in Suster, *The Occult Messiah,* p. 97.

8. Alan Bullock, *Hitler and Stalin: Parallel Lives* (London: HarperCollins, 1991), p. 150.

9. David Sampson, article in *Sydney Morning Herald,* 15 April 1989, pp. 87–88.

10. Harry M. Geduld, article in *U.S. Humanist,* January/February 1989, pp. 39–40.

11. Fest, *Hitler,* p. 189.

12. Ibid., p. 11.

13. Ibid., p. 24.

14. Bullock, *Hitler and Stalin: Parallel Lives,* p. 410.

Part One

Hitler and the Occult

1

Springtime for Hitler

Adolf Hitler was born in the Austrian border town of Branau on the River Inn 20 April 1889. At the time his birth was not hailed as the nativity of the leader of the master race, the coming of the *Volkisch** Messiah. Wise men did not congregate.

However, one writer asserts he may have literally drunk in occultic powers with his earliest milk. The same woman who wet-nursed Willi Schneinder, one of the noted psychic mediums of the time, also wet-nursed Hitler. Another who was also born in Branau was Madame Stockhammes.[1]

Occult historian Michael FitzGerald asks: Did Hitler grow up hearing stories about strange and scary powers—and decide to master them himself?[2] There is no strong body of evidence to support the assertion. However, the date of his birth was to take on an astrological significance, as we shall see.

Young Adolf's parents, Klara and Alois, were considered not so much normal as "ordinary" people. The father, an Austrian customs official, was apparently well respected in the community. Products of the late Victorian era, they observed the conventions of the time. Their child had to respect his elders and be loyal to his king and country. Clinical psychologist Edleff Schwaab, who specializes in abnormal psychology, finds that both parents

---

*"Intensely nationalistic"

were without apparent malice or inherent evilness in the way they brought up their son,[3] nor did Hitler himself show any early signs of possessing a sadistic streak.[4] In fact, Hitler's childhood is often dismissed as not worthy of lengthy analysis or comment in the context of what he was to become. For example, the prominent German psychoanalyst Alexander Mitcherlich says it did not provide any clues for the "monstrous development" of Hitler as a man of ruthless political suppression and murder.[5]

Bradley Smith, a war scholar who studied Hitler's early life, almost invites our sympathy when describing Adolf at this time: "[He] is a very human little boy . . . whose chief faults were his personal laziness and his passion for romantic games. He is someone we all know because we all have felt similar urges and experienced many of the same frustrations."[6]

Psychoanalyst Alice Miller paints a very different picture, one of a child brutalized from an early age by an overbearing father to such an extent that it was to have the most profound effect on his life:

> Little Adolf could be certain of receiving constant beatings; he knew nothing he did would have any affect on the daily thrashings he was given. All he could do was deny the pain, in other words, deny himself and identify with the aggressor. No one could help him, not even his mother, for this would spell danger for her too, she was also battered.[7]

Few of his biographers make much of the beatings the young Hitler received, accepting it as normal corporal punishment for the time. There appears to be a further reasoning to this: if a father's harsh discipline was blamed for Hitler's future behavior, why the world would be full of Hitlers! However, Miller's argument is that the beatings must not be seen in isolation but as part of a unique set of circumstances and timing relating specifically to Hitler.

As for his education, one of his teachers recalled in 1923 that Hitler had a high intelligence and definite talents but lacked discipline. He was, in fact, "notoriously cantankerous, willful, arrogant, and irascible."[8]

By the time Hitler entered secondary school in the Austrian provincial town of Linz, where the family had moved, his "attitude" had become a major problem. He continued to escape from anything resembling work in order to indulge his passion for playing war games and reading adventure novels.[9] His school reports continued to describe him in disparaging terms: idle, willful, and disrespectful.[10]

There has been speculation that at some stage of his childhood Hitler suffered a bout of epidemic encephalitis.[11] The form of this disease is known as encephalitis lethargia and it is now rare. Its cause is not known for certain. However, as its name suggests, it is colloquially called the "sleepy sickness" (as opposed to the "sleeping sickness").[12] The symptoms are fever, headache, irritability, and lethargy. In cases that recover there are residual deficiencies which improve only slowly and there may be permanent mental and neurological changes.[13] *The child victim may become unmanageable*[14] (which would account in large part for the descriptions of the young Hitler's behavior). In later years some patients develop symptoms of Parkinson's disease, which makes their limbs stiff in movement and shaky at rest.[15] This describes some of Hitler's physical problems toward the end of his life that are often attributed to other causes. Even if he did not reach the completely unmanageable stage, a bout of encephalitis would almost certainly have dramatically affected the character and personality of Adolf and also account for his difficulties at school.

Some contemporary occultic writers raise intriguing questions that they claim remain valid even now, fifty years after Hitler's death. How did he come to have such a formidable memory? Where did his intuitive powers originate? What was the source(s) of his mesmerizing oratory?

Hitler's memory was indeed impressive. According to his secretary, he could quote Arthur Schopenhauer by the page and other German philosophers who emphasized the power of will, including Friedrich Nietzsche, whose works were often on Hitler's lips.[16] Years later he could recall the serial number of the motorbike he rode during the First World War, and detailed facts and figures of military equipment such as tanks and ships with such assurance that senior officers were left dumbfounded—and impressed.[17]

However, there may be a more mundane—and very human—reason for his "extraordinary" mental powers: It is possible that Hitler had another potentially mentally crippling handicap, dyslexia.[18] Schwaab insists there is much evidence to indicate that Hitler was troubled by this severe learning disability.[19] If so, it can be assumed that Hitler sought to compensate in a way that many dyslexics do: by consciously developing oratorical skills. A naturally developed phenomenal memory is another compensatory gift often found in dyslexics. The evidence is not, however, conclusive, and Schwaab deals with it long after the deaths of those individuals who could personally confirm or deny it. However, it does challenge the view of Hitler being demoniacally gifted in these senses.

Alice Miller does not mention Hitler's physical problems in her thesis on his malformed character. Rather, she produces further evidence to show that his father was *the* root cause. When he was nearly eleven (the age at which he began to do poorly at school), Miller claims Adolf was almost beaten to death by his father when he tried to run away from home.[20] Having failed, he hit upon another way of rebelling: deliberately failing to achieve at school.[21]

Miller's assertion contradicts Joachim C. Fest, who argues that Hitler's poor academic performance had nothing to do with his relationship with his father, but was rather a result of increased academic demands in Linz. Fest asserts that the description of the allegedly prolonged conflict between Hitler and his father, which Hitler dramatized as a grim struggle between two men of iron will, has been exposed as pure fantasy.[22]

At secondary school Hitler was a total failure; in most subjects he scarcely received marks higher than "inadequate" or "adequate."[23] On the whole, his record was so poor that he left school.[24]

On 3 January 1903 Alois Hitler died suddenly from a stroke. Contrary to Fest's findings, Schwaab claims that Hitler, then thirteen, was upset at the loss of "what had been a strong, guiding influence in his life."[25] As a result he came to show signs of increasing self-isolation, inactivity, and depression.[26] On the other hand, Alan Bullock, another Hitler biographer, appears to back Fest's assertions when he says the death made no difference to Hitler's behavior, which had already been going from bad to worse.[27]

The secondary school in Linz may have been where he first tasted the bitter potion of racism, mixed with a decidedly nationalistic temper.[28] Pupils wore in their buttonholes the blue cornflower of Georg Ritter von Schonerer's Pan-German League, which was popular among German racist groups who also preferred the black-red-gold of the German unity movement rather than the Austrian colors. They greeted one another with the Germanic *Heil!*[29]

The school's history teacher, Dr. Leopold Potsch, is the first of a great number of racist-tainted persons said to have "deeply influenced" the young Hitler. Fest says unequivocally that Hitler's fundamental anti-Semitic attitudes undoubtedly came to him through Potsch.[30]

Although turn-of-the-century Vienna was a hotbed of anti-Semitism, hatred of Jews thrived to a lesser but still virulent degree in the provinces of the dying Austro-Hungarian Empire. Fanning those feelings in Linz was a largely satirical magazine specializing in attacks on Jews, papists, and other groups such as suffragists and members of parliament,[31] *Der Scherer Illustrierte Tiroler Monatsschrift für Politik und Launte in Kunst und Leben* (Illustrated Tyrolean Monthly for Politics and Entertainment in Art and Life).

The magazine may have the dubious distinction of providing Hitler with his initial idea for the symbol that was to become so uniquely and chillingly identified with his future Nazi party. It carried the swastika on its masthead to denote its empathy for the German *volkisch* (that is, racist and nationalistic attitudes).[32]

Whatever the reasons—illness, brutalization by his father, a warped personality, a too-high intelligence, a percipient nationalism having its basis in racism—Hitler as a teenager was drifting on troubled waters, sustained only by an overactive and unrealistic imagination.

Notes

1. Michael FitzGerald, *Storm Troopers of Satan* (London: Robert Hale, 1990), p. 13.

2. Ibid.

3. Edleff Schwaab, *Hitler's Mind: A Plunge into Madness* (New York: Praeger, 1992), p. 13.

4. Ibid., p. 66.

5. Ibid., p. 12.

6. Bradley Smith, *Adolf Hitler: His Family, Childhood and Youth* (Stanford, Calif.: Stanford University Press, 1967), p. 159.

7. Alice Miller, *For Your Own Good* (London: Virago Press, 1987), p. 162.

8. Werner Maser, *Hitler: Legend, Myth and Reality* (New York: Harper & Row, 1973), p. 125.

9. Alan Bullock, *Hitler and Stalin: Parallel Lives* (HarperCollins, 1991), p. 7.

10. Ibid.

11. Schwaab, *Hitler's Mind,* p. 96, n. 1.

12. *Pears Medical Encyclopedia* (London: Pelham Books, 1977), p. 143.

13. Ibid.

14. Ibid.

15. Ibid.

16. Trevor-Roper in his introduction to *Hitler's Table Talk 1941–44,* trans. Norman Cameron and R. H. Stevens (London: Weidenfeld and Nicholson, 1953).

17. Schwaab, *Hitler's Mind,* pp. 30–31.

18. Ibid., p. 96.

19. Ibid., p. 97.

20. Miller, *For Your Own Good,* p. 168, n. 5.

21. Ibid., p. 168.

22. Joachim C. Fest, *Hitler* (Hammondsworth, Middlesex, U.K.: Pelican Books, 1977), p. 32.

23. Ibid., p. 31.

24. Ibid.

25. Schwaab, *Hitler's Mind,* p. 97, n. 1.

26. Ibid., p. 97.

27. Bullock, *Hitler and Stalin,* p. 7.

28. Fest, *Hitler,* p. 59.
29. Ibid., p. 59.
30. Ibid.
31. Ibid., p. 60.
32. Ibid.

2

Hitler's Erratic Search

In mid-1907 Hitler persuaded his mother that he should seek a new direction by becoming a student at the Vienna Academy of Arts. As his father had once done, he set out from his home village for the city vowing not to return until he had made something of himself.[1]

However, instead of sitting for the admission exams he became a dropout, aimlessly enjoying the Austrian capital, indulging his imagination, and giving free rein to his passion for escaping any responsibilities. He did not usually rise until noon, then he would saunter the streets or parks and visit museums, art galleries, and the like. At night he would often attend the opera.[2] He dressed as a young man of leisure carrying an ivory-topped black cane, giving every indication he was a university student.[3]

Hitler in this period painted only occasionally, water colors filled with finicky detail that betrayed nothing of the forces raging within him.[4] He spent far more time indulging in extravagant daydreams of how he would one day overwhelm the world with his deeds.[5] His friend August Kubizek from Linz, a music student who lived in lodgings with Hitler for a while in Vienna, found him to be completely out of control: states of exaltation alternated with moods of deep depression in which he saw nothing but injustice, hatred, and hostility directed against him. In his depressions he would rail against the whole of humanity; it did not understand him, would not accept him; it persecuted and cheated him and set snares for the sole purpose of preventing him from getting somewhere.[6]

Nevertheless he illogically believed that destiny had a special future role for him—at first it was to be that of an artistic genius. However, when he did finally sit for the art school exams, "full of confidence and self-assurance," he failed.[7] The school records note: "The following gentlemen submitted unsatisfactory drawings or were not admitted to the examination . . . Adolf Hitler, Branau a. Inn, 20 April 1889, German, Catholic, Father civil servant, upper rank. Four grades of Realschule. Few heads. Sample drawing unsatisfactory."[8] Hitler notes that, "I was so convinced I had been successful that when I received my rejection it struck me as a bolt from the blue . . . a lightning flash."[9]

No doubt, based at least partly on the examiner's terse report, the cause of Hitler's failure is given by a number of his biographers, including Alan Bullock, as the fact that he was not good enough, even that the very idea of his applying was another of his grandiose notions without foundation. Bullock says Hitler continued to delude himself throughout his life that he was an artistic genius, frequently lamenting what the world had lost when, out of a sense of duty, he was forced to turn to politics.[10]

In fact the entrance standard was high: only 28 of the 120 applicants who sat had been accepted. The German author Wulf Schwarzwaller* says it would be completely wrong to conclude that Hitler was less talented than the successful applicants: the decision to accept or reject an applicant was at times arbitrary and subjective. Many of the applicants who were originally accepted for being "highly talented" later sank into obscurity while some of those who failed the same examination—as Hitler did—went on to make a name for themselves as professional artists.[11]

Hitler's sketches contained outstandingly rendered details of streets and buildings but there was an almost total absence of people or animals; where he did depict them they looked more

---

*His other books include *Rudolf Hess the Deputy* (London: Quartet Books, 1988).

like puppets, while the trees were more plastic-cast scenery than living organisms.[12] It can be assumed that one important reason the judges were put off was the absence of life forms in his work.

Hitler sought an interview with the school director over his rejection. It was suggested that his talents lay in architecture, not painting. However, Hitler did not bother to follow up on the suggestion.[13] Instead, he turned his seething mind to other areas that could do with the help of his unrecognized genius.

> He developed a scheme for a nonalcoholic drink; he looked for substitutes for smoking or drew up plans for the reform of schools. He composed theses attacking landlords and officials (and) outlines for a "German ideal state."[14]

Hitler also read a diverse range of books and attended lectures on all sorts of subjects including the occult. According to August Kubizek, a friend of the young Hitler, Hitler's interests included Oriental religion, astrology, yoga, hypnotism, and other aspects of occultism.[15] Other writers, such as Francis King (*Satan and Swastika*), Gerald Suster (*Hitler: The Occult Messiah*), and Trevor Ravenscroft (*The Spear of Destiny*), obviously hoping to tie Hitler closely to the occult, specifically add numerology, magic, the paranormal, psychokinesis, water divining, graphology, numerology, physiognomy, and many other offbeat subjects.

Conventional historian Hugh Trevor-Roper comes up with a different list of Hitler's reading material for this period: books on history and religion, on geography and technology, art history and architecture, and Karl von Clauswitz, the acknowledged genius of military science.[16]

These contrasting lists give us no sense of balance or preference in Hitler's reading. The pro- and anti-occult writers do not help. All we do know is that Hitler's avid if undisciplined reading in this period of his life helped shape his character and the beliefs which he was to hold so unshakably for the rest of his life.

He was certainly a voracious reader—Hitler claimed he had read all five hundred assorted volumes in one Viennese bookstore[17]—which, if true, very much weakens the "evidence" that

Hitler suffered from dyslexia,[18] unless we are to hypothesize that he read largely for effect and the dyslexic difficulty he experienced, rather than any intellectual impairment, was behind his inability to critically absorb and evaluate much of the material.

In all, Hitler lived in Vienna for six years, from 1907 to 1913, and later painted a picture of hardship and misery in which he was forced to work as a laborer and a small-time painter with hunger always present. Occult author Trevor Ravenscroft, for example, talks of Hitler at this stage as being dressed in a sleazy overcoat far too large for him, with his toes visible through a crack in his shoes beneath frayed trouser ends, trying to sell his postcard paintings to passing tourists, and living in a flophouse.[19] Smith, who studied Hitler's early life, writes of Hitler as a young adult struggling in Vienna, a sympathetic figure more threatened by than threatening to the social order in which he eked out an existence.[20] However, Fest argues that at least for the first part of this period of his life, Hitler was quite comfortable thanks to a share in his father's inheritance, his mother's legacy (she died in December 1907), and an orphan pension.[21] Hitler himself, conveniently forgetting the times he roamed the city at will and lived a life of leisure and irresponsibility, describes Vienna as "the hardest though most thorough school of my life." Here he learned all he needed to know to assume control of the Nazi party in later years: a worldview (*Weltanschauung*) formed in his mind which became the granite foundation of his future decision making, and although he later needed to supplement it in detail, it never left him.[22]

Several writers note the influence on the young Hitler of anti-Semitic Viennese politicians of the time such as Georg Ritter von Schonerer of the Pan-German League and Dr. Karl Lueger of the Christian Socialists. Lueger was the mayor of Vienna for four of the five years Hitler spent there. Schwaab attributes much of Hitler's "peculiar thinking about racism and nationalism" to these politicians together with his compulsive reading about socialism, Judaism, and Marxism.[23]

Hitler lived for a while on the street where von Schonerer's newspaper was published and the frequency with which some of

the newspaper's pet terms for Vienna—such as "ethnic conglo-
merate" and "ethnic Babylon"—appear later in *Mein Kampf* has
led to the conclusion that Hitler read the paper regularly in addition
to the equally racist *Ostara* magazine.[24]

As for Hitler's anti-Semitism, in Vienna it had become an
overwhelming phobia.[25] The British occult historian Francis King
offers a pragmatic explanation for its virulence at this time: It
may have been to some extent because Hitler so desperately needed
someone to hate as a psychological antidote to his own miseries.
Taking up Hitler's poignant picture of himself in Vienna, King
goes on to say that "when one is physically hungry and emotionally
deprived—and the young Hitler was usually both—it is a great
comfort to have some group of people . . . who can be blamed
for what is profoundly one's own fault." A further reason for his
hatred, King adds, is that Hitler may have been defeated in love
by some Jewish rivals; or perhaps had acquired syphilis or some
other venereal disease from a Jewish girl.

In any case, he goes on, it is probable Hitler had some sort
of sexual motive for his hatred of the Jews.

King bases his assumptions on certain passages from *Mein
Kampf* including one in which Hitler writes of a black-haired Jewish
youth lying in wait for and "satanically . . . spying upon the un-
suspecting girl whom he plans to seduce, adulterating her blood
and removing her from her own people."

Such passages, says King, associate disease with racial de-
generacy and, at the same time, convey a depth of feeling which
seem to reveal a certain personal anguish.[26] However, he provides
no other proof which would lead us to believe Hitler was syphilitic
at any stage of his life.

It could be argued that Hitler's anti-Semitism was based not
on logic or resentment or jealousy or even VD, but on perversity.
For example, from what is known of Hitler to that stage of his
life, the Jewish question should have been the last thing on his
mind. Hitler's early contacts with Jews had been limited but re-
markably positive. Jews had been among his benefactors. A Jewish
doctor had treated his mother's breast cancer without payment.

Most of the paintings he sold in Vienna went to three Jewish art dealers who encouraged his efforts. He had received help from Jewish-financed charities and made some Jewish friends in the flophouses.[27]

Two things in particular did incite Hitler's hatred of the Jews in Vienna. First, they appeared to control the theater, the film industry, and the media in general. He began to see the press as a gigantic conspiracy that criticized German authors and artists while favoring their Jewish counterparts. Second, Jews controlled much of Vienna's Social Democratic party. Hitler despised socialists, not because of their advocacy but because they espoused the internationalism of the world socialist movement, which alarmed Hitler who had been an ardent German nationalist since his time at the Linz secondary school. The fact that the Jews were so deeply involved with socialism offered further proof to Hitler of their non-nationalist, and therefore non-German, character.[28]

In a paradoxical twist Alice Miller says the allegations that Hitler had a Jewish ancestry may provide the clue to his anti-Semitism. She says it weighed on his father, Alois, throughout his life that he was not only illegitimate and separated from his real mother at the age of five, but that his unknown father may have been Jewish, which in Alois's surroundings meant disgrace and isolation.[29] As a result he took out the resulting frustrations cruelly on his son. Hitler in turn took out his hatred of his sadistic father by transferring it to the Jews in later life. They became the bearer of all the evil and despicable traits the child had ever observed in his overbearing father. Alois was the hated Jew whom he could despise and persecute, frighten and threaten with regulations: the racial laws were meant to mark Hitler's final break with his father and his background.[30]

Miller's thesis battles for space in the vast forest of material seeking to explain, often far more dramatically and expansively than she does, the "Hitler Phenomenon." Much of what passes as explanation is speculative, sensational, or imagination in free flight. On the other hand, her assertion has a compelling ring to it and a compulsive simplicity.

Rumor and conjecture about Hitler's Jewishness dogged him from early in his rise to power. A story in the United Kingdom's *Daily Mirror* on 14 October 1933 helped greatly in fueling the speculation.[31] A journalist had found a grave in the Jewish cemetery in Bucharest which was inscribed with Hebrew characters "Adolf Hitler." The *Mirror* alleged that the grave belonged to the grandfather of "Germany's anti-Semitic chancellor." The story was taken up by publications around the world, although within Germany itself with Hitler in power such speculation had ceased to be in the public domain. According to Werner Maser, the postwar German author of a number of books on Hitler, the headstone and death certificate gave this Hitler's birth date as 1832, which would make him only five years older than Adolf's father, therefore he could not possibly have been Hitler's grandfather.[32]

However, the most compelling claim for Hitler's ancestry came eighteen months after his death in the Berlin bunker. Hans Frank, who had been Hitler's legal adviser and Governor-General of Poland from 1939 to 1945, was facing the gallows at the Nuremberg trials and declared he did not want to leave behind any "unatoned guilt" (he had embraced Catholicism in prison). As part of his confession he wrote a document in which he said that toward the end of 1930 he had, at Hitler's request, made some confidential inquiries into a letter Hitler had received from a relative which Hitler declared amounted to a "disgusting piece of blackmail." The letter claimed that Hitler had Jewish blood in his veins! Frank's inquiries elicited the information that Hitler's father was the illegitimate son of a woman by the name of Maria Anna Schicklgruber from Leonding, near Linz (in Austria), who worked as a cook. When she gave birth to Alois she was in service with a Jewish family by the name of Frankenberger. On behalf of his son, who had been about nineteen years old, Frankenberger paid a maintenance allowance to Schicklgruber from the time of the child's birth until his fourteenth year. Hence, Frank concluded in his document, the possibility could not be dismissed that Hitler's father was half-Jewish as a result of the extramarital relationship between Schicklgruber and the Jew from Graz.[33] If so, Hitler was one-quarter Jewish.

Had Frank's story become known in the 1930s, Hitler's career would obviously have been in deep trouble. Even when the document was released in the early fifties it "preoccupied a whole generation of biographers, and fired their imaginations."[34]

Maser investigated the claims and found that none of Frank's statements withstood close analysis.[35] There was no evidence that a Jew by the name of Frankenberger lived in Austria throughout the nineteenth century. In Graz itself he was unable to find that one single Jew had lived there from the fifteenth century until 100 years after Maria Anna's death. No records showed she was employed in any Graz household in 1836 or 1837. Her name is not recorded in the town's Servant Register or its Citizens Register.[36]

In fact Maria Anna gave birth to Alois on 7 June 1837, in Strones, near Doellersheim and when asked who the father was she refused to say.[37] At the time of her death Maria Anna was forty-two years old. Alois was her first and only child. The father was almost certainly Johann Nepomuk Huettler.[38] Five years after Alois's birth, in a bizarre twist, she married Johann Nepomuk's brother Johann Georg, a carpenter. Johann Georg could not stand having an illegitimate child around the house so at the age of five young Alois was sent to live with his real father,[39] a move which Miller claims traumatized the boy. (It is Frank's story which Miller appears to accept.)

At the age of eighteen Alois joined the customs service (the Imperial and Royal Finance Guard) and advanced rapidly. But in his early thirties he still worried that his illegitimacy might hinder his further advancement in the bureaucracy. To help him overcome the problem, Johann Nepomuk told the pastor at Doellersheim that Johann Georg had admitted in front of witnesses before he died that he was the father of Alois. When the pastor came to make an entry in the register to this effect, thus legitimizing Alois, he apparently misheard Johann Nepomuk pronounce his surname and wrote down "Hitler."[40] Thus the name that was to terrify the world came into being.

Maser would appear to have the evidence to back up his denial of Hitler's Jewish ancestry. But a doubt must remain. Why would Frank, faced with monstrous crimes and apparently under the guidance of an American Franciscan Army chaplain, deny himself atonement when given a final chance for it?[41] Maser offers a justification for such arch deviousness: Frank may have been seeking not only to disembarrass his fellow Catholics for Adolf Hitler, the Catholic mass-murderer, but also to foment unrest, anxiety, and a lasting sense of guilt among "the Jews."[42] The explanation has a compelling if awful consistency.

As for Hitler's own thoughts on the matters, he claims in *Mein Kampf* and elsewhere that his anti-Semitism grew as a gradual process, the impression being that it was based on objective, rather than subjective reasons, good cause rather than bias, and certainly not on childhood emotions.

There is agreement between orthodox and occult historians that in 1909 Hitler came under the influence of a Lanz Von Liebenfels, a defrocked monk who was not only an astrologer, but a racist whose real name was Adolf Lanz. Some occult writers see this as part of a process in which Hitler drifted deeper if irrationally into occult studies.

Ravenscroft, for example, has him at this time making a penetrating study of medieval occultism and ritual magic and taking drugs to attain higher levels of consciousness.[43] Suster says the young Hitler was experimenting with occultic exercises that enhance the faculties and lead to states of transcendent consciousness using as his guide ponderous and verbose occultic writings from which he extracted scraps of methods, not caring whether his sources advocated good or evil. As a result of these esoteric studies Hitler's inner life was transformed beyond his expectations—he had arrived at some mysterious knowledge which assured him of a place in the history books.[44]

The extent of Liebenfel's influence is contested. Francis King says the ex-monk exerted a major intellectual influence upon Hitler.[45] Long before the First World War, Liebenfels had been publicly advocating the desirability of some of the most unpleasant measures later adopted by Hitler: for example, the imprisonment and forcible sterilization of "socially inferior elements," and

heavy penalties for those indulging in interracial sexual relationships.[46]

> Indeed, it would be hardly going too far to say that the hor-
> rors of Belsen and the ovens of Auschwitz were ultimately de-
> rived from the occult-racial ravings of von Liebenfels and the
> tiny group of his followers who existed like maggots on an
> apple.[47]

Liebenfels founded an occult secret society, the New Templars, around 1894 but it appears not to have grown until he built
his first temple, on the banks of the Danube in 1907. From the
newly completed temple Liebenfels hoisted the swastika flag—the
sign which stood for all he believed in: "an abandonment of Christianity, an embracing of neo-paganism, a desire to become or create
the superman, and an affirmation of Aryan racial superiority."[48]
    The swastika was a well-known Nordic sign. However, it gained
modern fame—or infamy—as a result of Hitler adopting it as the
symbol of the Nazi party (see chapter 12).
    Liebenfels produced the *Ostara* which carried on its masthead
the swastika and the slogan "the Blond Fighters of the Rights
of Man." Its answer to the so-called Jewish problem was the
castration knife.[49]
    The claim that Hitler was a reader of *Ostara* must be qualified
by doubts about the extent of his interest in the magazine's material.
It did serve as an introduction to Liebenfels in 1909 when Hitler
called at its office to buy some back issues.[50]
    Further "evidence" of a Hitler-Liebenfels connection is found
in a 1932 letter written by Liebenfels and quoted as corroboration
for such a connection by both Francis King[51] and Gerald Suster,
a pro-occult writer.[52] The letter to a New Templar initiate says,
"Hitler is one of our pupils. . . . [Y]ou will one day experience
that he, and through him we, will one day be victorious and develop
a movement that will make the world tremble."
    On the surface all this appears to be reasonable evidence of
Hitler's involvement with the defrocked monk in what Suster calls
the "novel and strange, irrational, and repellent" atmosphere that

was the German-speaking world of the occult in the early twentieth century.[53] But does the evidence stand up?

Fest, for one, thinks not. The renowned biographer of Hitler summarizes Liebenfels as "rather ludicrous." As far as Hitler being a pupil of Liebenfels's, the occultist also named Lord Kitchener and V. I. Lenin as among his pupils![54]

Edleff Schwaab also believes that too much has been made of the impact of Liebenfels. Hitler may have known of him and may have read his *Ostara* magazine in moments of curiosity but there are simply no indications to assume that Hitler aspired to be part of Liebenfels's racial-spirit nonsense. Moreover Hitler saw himself functioning on a much higher mental level producing ideas so advanced that they could not be fully comprehended by mere mortals—there was no room in them for the world of Liebenfels.[55]

To summarize, we have a hodgepodge of influences on Hitler at this stage of his life: His hedonistic lifestyle in Vienna, followed by a touch of poverty; his extravagant daydreams and immature mood swings; his warped worldview in which he, a "misunderstood genius," was nevertheless a victim of imagined injustices; his failure in art, followed by his failure to make the effort to formally study architecture; his wide-ranging, yet indiscriminate reading; anti-Semitic politicians; the obvious influence of Jews on so many aspects of Vienna's lifestyle, which served to stir Hitler's incipient nationalism; memories of his father (was young Adolf aware of the Jewish connection in his background?); and finally, the claims of occult influences, its philosophy in harness with racist dogmas. All this and we have not yet considered the greatest alleged influence of them all on Hitler: the Holy Lance.

Notes

1. Joachim C. Fest, *Hitler* (Hammondsworth, Middlesex, U.K.: Pelican Books, 1977), p. 38.

2. Ibid., p. 48.

3. Alan Bullock, *Hitler and Stalin: Parallel Lives* (London: HarperCollins, 1991), p. 7.

4. Fest, *Hitler,* p. 49, n. 1.

5. Bullock, *Hitler and Stalin,* p. 7, n. 3.

6. Fest, *Hitler,* p. 50.

7. Adolf Hitler, *Mein Kampf* (London: Hutchinson, 1974), p. 18.

8. Fest, *Hitler,* p. 44.

9. Hitler, *Mein Kampf,* p. 18, n. 7.

10. Bullock, *Hitler and Stalin,* p. 7, n. 3.

11. Wulf Schwarzwaller, *The Unknown Hitler* (Bethesda, Md.: Zenith, 1989), p. 24.

12. Ibid., pp. 24–25.

13. Bullock, *Hitler and Stalin,* p. 8.

14. Fest, *Hitler,* p. 49.

15. Francis King, *Satan and Swastika* (St. Albans, Herts, U.K.: Mayflower Books, 1976), p. 107.

16. Hugh Trevor-Roper in his foreword to *Hitler's Table Talk 1941–44,* trans. Norman Cameron and R. H. Stevens (London: Weidenfeld and Nicholson, 1953), p. xxxix.

17. Ibid. p. xxviii.

18. Edleff Schwaab, *Hitler's Mind: A Plunge into Madness* (New York: Praeger, 1992), p. 96 (see ch. 6).

19. Trevor Ravenscroft, *The Spear of Destiny* (York Beach, Me.: Samuel Weiser Inc., 1982), pp. 54–56.

20. Bradley Smith, *Adolf Hitler: His Family, Childhood and Youth* (Stanford, Calif.: Stanford University Press, 1967), p. 159.

21. Fest, *Hitler,* p. 48.

22. Hitler, *Mein Kampf,* p. 114.

23. Schwaab, *Hitler's Mind,* p. 110, n. 15.

24. George Berkley, *Vienna and Its Jews* (Cambridge, Mass.: Abt Books, 1988), p. 110.

25. Fest, *Hitler,* p. 63.

26. King, *Satan and Swastika,* pp. 106–107, n. 12.

27. Berkley, *Vienna and Its Jews,* p. 109, n. 20.

28. Ibid., p. 110.

29. Alice Miller, *For Your Own Good* (London: Virago Press, 1987), pp. 150–51.

30. Ibid., p. 178.

31. Quoted in Werner Maser, *Hitler: Legend, Myth and Reality,* trans. Peter and Betty Ross (New York: Harper & Row, 1973), p. 10.

32. Ibid.

33. Ibid., pp. 11–12.

34. Ibid., pp. 13–14.

35. Ibid., p. 14.

36. Ibid., p. 11.

37. Schwarzwaller, *The Unknown Hitler,* p. 12, n. 11.

38. Ibid., p. 12.

39. Ibid.

40. Ibid., pp. 12–13.

41. Maser, *Hitler,* p. 11.

42. Ibid., p. 14.

43. King, *Satan and Swastika,* p. xxi.

44. Gerald Suster, *Hitler: The Occult Messiah* (New York: St. Martin's Press, 1981), pp. 51–52.

45. King, *Satan and Swastika,* p. 65.

46. Ibid.

47. Ibid.

48. Gerald *Hitler: The Occult Messiah,* p. 25.

49. Ibid., p. 35.

50. King, *Satan and Swastika,* p. 79.

51. Ibid., p. 80.

52. Suster, *Hitler,* p. 36. Both King and Suster use the same source: Wilfried Daim, *Der Mann der Hitler die Idean gab* (The Man Who Gave Hitler the Ideas) (Munich, 1958).

53. Ibid., p. 36.

54. Fest, *Hitler,* p. 1140.

55. Schwaab, *Hitler's Mind,* p. 66.

3

Hitler Discovers the Holy Lance

The most controversial book of the year. I think it could become
an all-time best seller.

> Colin Wilson's comment on *The Spear of Destiny*[1]

The talisman of power (the Holy Lance) . . . was to become
the central pivot in the life of Adolf Hitler and the very source
of his ambitions to conquer the world.

> Trevor Ravenscroft[2]

The Holy Lance is said to have been used by a Roman centurion
(soldier) to pierce the side of Jesus Christ as he hung from the
cross. A number of relics held in churches and other holy places
in Europe are claimed to be the genuine lance. The lance in the
Weltliches Schatzkammer Museum (Hapsburg Treasure House
Museum) in Vienna has been there for most of the past 250-odd
years. It is also known as the Lance of St. Maurice, or Constantine's
Lance, and was used as a symbol of the imperial power of Holy
Roman emperors at the time of their coronation much as the
orb and scepter play a symbolic role in the coronations of British
monarchs.

The way Trevor Ravenscroft tells the story in *The Spear of
Destiny,* nineteen-year-old Adolf Hitler was led to the Holy Lance
in a providential experience in Vienna in 1908. The catalyst is
seen as his physical and mental state: cold and miserable outside

the museum, he was also broke, hungry, and alone. It was raining, and his sketchbook had been soaked in the early autumn drizzle. In a stabbing moment of reality "he saw that all his grandiose architectural plans into which he had thrown himself body and soul, were utterly worthless." Tearing up his sketchbook in disgust he walked into the museum looking for warmth and shelter and the possibility that he might be able to reassess his hopeless situation.[3] (The picture of Hitler throwing his energies into architectural interests at this time is a clear contradiction of Bullock's version of Hitler's attitude as a result of his failure to gain entrance into the art school. As we saw in the previous chapter, the school's director had suggested to Hitler that his talents lay in architecture, not painting. Hitler lacked the school-leaving certificate necessary to start on a course of professional training in architecture, but if he had been serious it would not have been a problem to secure this. However, he did not even bother to find out what was required. Instead, he continued with his feverish but aimless activity in Vienna.[4])

Ravenscroft does not explain why Hitler would expect to find such disparate needs as warmth, shelter, and philosophical insights in the museum. Hitler had visited it often and obviously it met his physical needs for warmth on a cold day. But he had never found the exhibits fulfilling other needs. In fact, he thought most of the objects meaningless junk.[5]

Hitler was standing in front of the display containing the lance when a tour party comprising foreign politicians arrived. He did not listen at first, merely regarding their presence as "an intrusion into the privacy of my own despairing thoughts." Then he heard the words "which were to change my whole life": *"There is a legend associated with this Spear that whoever claims it, and solves its secret, holds the destiny of the world in his hands for good or evil."*[6] The lance that was holding the attention of Hitler and the tourists consists of two parts held together by a golden sheath. Inserted into one part, the blade or spearhead, is a nail said to be from Christ's cross and held in place with gold, silver, and copper threads. The base of the lance is embossed with two gold crosses.

The guide went on to say that Napoleon Bonaparte, the only person who had given the legend credence for the past five hundred or so years, had demanded the lance after the battle of Austerlitz (a town in Moravia, now in the Czech nation). The battle took place on 2 December 1805. Just before the battle began, the lance had been smuggled out of Nuremberg and hidden in Vienna to keep it out of the French dictator's hands.[7]

Here we have a clear inconsistency with known facts: Vienna would not have been a logical choice as a hiding place for the lance; the French had occupied the city on 10 November 1805, weeks before the battle began. They were still in occupation on 2 December.[8] Why would anyone want to smuggle anything into an occupied city if the purpose in so doing was to keep it out of the hands of the head of the occupying force? In any case, attested historical records show that the lance was taken from Nuremberg and brought to Vienna in 1800, not 1805, and was on display in the museum. Therefore, had he wanted the lance, Napoleon had no need to wait until after the battle, nor was the lance hidden from him. As this example shows, the best thing that can be said about Ravenscroft's use of dates is that it is lackadaisical. Returning to the museum, despite the guide's qualified claim, it appears that Hitler became an instant convert.

> I knew with immediacy that this was an important moment in my life. . . . It seemed to carry some hidden inner meaning which evaded me, a meaning which I felt I inwardly knew yet could not bring to consciousness. . . . The [lance] appeared to be some sort of magical medium of revelation. . . . I felt as though I myself had held it in my hands before in some earlier century of history—that I myself had once claimed it as my talisman of power and held the destiny of the world in my hands. Yet how could this be possible? What sort of madness was this that was invading my mind and creating such turmoil in my breast?[9]

There appears to be only Ravenscroft's word that this encounter between Hitler and the lance took place. Substantial doubts arise as to the authenticity of the actual words attributed to Hitler. Ravenscroft uses phrases such as "Hitler later recounted" and "he said later" in his attribution of these comments, without noting to whom Hitler was speaking, or even how much later, or where. Ravenscroft's own phraseology in this context reminds us of expressions from the legend of *Parsifal,* such as "as I heard it told," expressions which have given rise to questions as to the source of Wolfram von Eschenbach's twelfth-century romance (see chapter 9, "Hitler and *Parsifal*").

Ravenscroft cites some passages as taken from the book written by August Kubizek, Hitler's only known friend at this time. This provides a clue. Ravenscroft calls Kubizek "the only other reliable witness" to Hitler's life at this time.[10] So the first "reliable witness" has to be the person to whom Hitler allegedly poured out his heart about the affects of his confrontation with the lance, a person who Ravenscroft initially does not name. That person turns out to be Ravenscroft's mentor, Dr. Walter Stein. However, when Ravenscroft admits this later in his book, he goes on to *deny* the accuracy of the earlier quotes, which he initially uses so authoritatively, saying there is no written record of the "exact dialogue" between Stein and Hitler, simply "the sequence of events which took place at their spasmodic meetings."[11]

Stein, we are told, gave Ravenscroft details of the conversations between Hitler and himself in the late forties and early fifties, nearly forty years after they are said to have occurred.[12] In addition, Ravenscroft admits he took no verbatim notes or tape recordings of Stein's words at this time, making only general comments in his diaries, claiming that he had no idea that the task of writing *Spear* would fall to him.[13] Ravenscroft uses the quotes in such a confusing way that the credibility of the whole story as a factual work can only be considered doubtful.

Conveniently for Ravenscroft, Hitler left very little in the way of personal, documented material that may have enabled us to make some basic comparisons with what Ravenscroft alleges. As we know from the hoax of the eighties, he did not keep diaries. We can learn little from his book *Mein Kampf,* which became the Nazi "Bible" and which was summed up by the occult writer Suster[14] as a succession of rambling, banal, and intensely wearisome monologues by a thoroughly third-rate mind. The British historian Bullock[15] trenchantly comments that *Mein Kampf* has few rivals in the repulsiveness of its language, its tone, and above all its contents.

Few writers claim—as Ravenscroft does for Stein—to have had recorded private conversations with Hitler. An examination of two men who did and lived to tell their stories is highly revealing in helping us get to the veracity of Ravenscroft's material. One is Nazi renegade Hermann Rauschning, the other being one of Hitler's former confidants, Otto Wagener. When we examine the circumstances surrounding the gathering and recording of their material we find paradoxical similarities with those cited by Ravenscroft for his Hitler conversation material.

The German historian Theodore Schieder[16] has observed that Rauschning in his book *Hitler Speaks* (London: Butterworth, 1939) employed direct discourse as a literary form, not as a means of precisely replicating the quoted words, which is the way we are forced to evaluate the Ravenscroft quotes. Rauschning[17] wrote down his material five to seven years after his conversations with Hitler are said to have occurred.

As with Rauschning, Wagener's material also cannot be regarded as a verbatim account despite the fact that he was with Hitler literally hundreds of times, often unaccompanied by others. Wagener produced his memoirs fourteen to seventeen years after the period in question relying on his memory. He claimed to have kept a spasmodic diary during the years of his encounters with Hitler between 1929–33. Most of the diary had been damaged or destroyed during the war. In any case he composed his memoirs while a prisoner-of-war in Britain so he did not have access to the surviving part of such a diary.

In neither case did the men ever produce the notations they claimed to have made and these notes were never seen by anyone else. As we have seen, Ravenscroft[18] did not make notes of his conversations with Stein, whose memory of his conversations with Hitler had to stretch back much further than either Rauschning and Wagener—more than thirty years. One further source for direct quotes is *Hitler's Table Talk 1941-44** which consists of even more monologues of Hitler's, on a wide variety of subjects. Much of it is banal and contains few insights into Hitler's *raison.*

In his frenzied search for the history of the object that had so excited him, Ravenscroft tells us Hitler found little difficulty in sorting out the merits of the various lances "purporting to be the weapon of the Roman centurion [who Ravenscroft says was named Gaius Cassius[19]] which were scattered around the palaces, museums, cathedrals, and churches of Europe and was excited to find one spear which appeared to have been associated with a legend of world destiny throughout its entire history."[20]

Here ambiguity arises, for Ravenscroft says in this passage that this lance dates back only to the third century! This raises the obvious question: If so, how could this be the authentic Holy Lance? It is a question Ravenscroft[21] does not address when talking of the dating of the lance. However, in later pages he unambiguously states that the lance Hitler stood before in the museum was the "Spear of Longinus" (Longinus being another name for Cassius, the centurion)—that is, the Holy Lance,[22] and reiterates that it was *the* weapon thrust into the side of Jesus while he hung on the cross.[23]

In his search for information, Hitler found a number of the famous men who had been owners of the lance: Constantine, Charlemagne, and Frederick the Great of Germany who founded the Teutonic Knights[24] (on which Hitler's SS was supposedly based).

Altogether forty-five emperors claimed the Holy Lance as their possession between Charlemagne's coronation in Rome and the fall of the old German Empire exactly one thousand years later.[25]

It is difficult to deal with the claim that many famous leaders had a lance, if not *the* lance, in their possession, which they regarded with varying degrees of importance and influence: the Orb and Sceptre are important symbols of Britain's royal line, however they do not feature large in the history of that family.

---

*N. Cameron and R. H. Stevens, *Hitler's Table Talk 1941-44* (London: Wiedenfeld and Nicholson, 1953).

In summary, the inconsistencies, inaccuracies, and paradoxes I have revealed make it difficult to understand how Colin Wilson, the distinguished writer on the occult and diverse other matters, came to give Ravenscroft's book the accolade mentioned at the start of this chapter.

Before continuing with the story of Hitler and the Holy Lance, we need to attempt, briefly, to trace its origins as well as historical and religious significance if any.

Notes

1. Promotion lines on cover of hardcover edition of Trevor Ravenscroft, *The Spear of Destiny* (New York: G. P. Putnam & Sons, 1973).

2. Trevor Ravenscroft, *The Spear of Destiny* (York Beach, Me.: Samuel Weiser Inc., 1991), p. 61.

3. Ibid., p. 6.

4. Alan Bullock, *Hitler and Stalin: Parallel Lives* (London: HarperCollins, 1991), pp. 8–9.

5. Ravenscroft, *The Spear of Destiny,* p. 7.

6. Ibid.

7. Ibid., p. 8.

8. David Chandler, *Napoleon* (London: Purnell, 1973), pp. 71–72.

9. Ravenscroft, *The Spear of Destiny,* pp. 8–9.

10. Ibid., p. xxi.

11. Ibid., p. 60.

12. Ibid., p. xx–xxi.

13. Ibid., p. 60.

14. Gerald Suster, *Hitler: The Occult Messiah* (New York: St. Martin's Press, 1981), p. 119.

15. Bullock, *Hitler and Stalin,* p. 157.

16. Cited by Henry Ashby Turner, English language editor of Otto Wagener, *Hitler: Memoirs of a Confidant* (New Haven, Conn.: Yale University Press, 1978), p. xv.

17. Ibid., p. xvi.

18. Ravenscroft, *The Spear of Destiny,* p. 60.

19. Ibid., p. 12.

20. Ibid.

21. Ibid., pp. 32 and 37.
22. Ibid., p. 63.
23. Ibid., p. 14.
24. Ibid., pp. 16–17.
25. Ibid.

4

The Bible and the Holy Lance

The Crucifixion and Resurrection of Jesus are of pivotal importance to Christianity for the promise they hold out to believers. "When God calleth you to come unto Christ, he promiseth that the virtue of Christ's death shall kill sin in you, and the virtue of Christ's Resurrection shall raise you up to the newness of life."[1] These words are easily understood as the same article of faith by today's Christians as by the parishioners addressed by seventeenth-century preacher John Preston and understood equally well by the Christians who preceded Preston by centuries.

However, the role of the Holy Lance in the story of the Crucifixion and Resurrection does not carry such certainties. To put that role into context we take up the story of Jesus at the height of his "career" riding into Jerusalem on an ass and proclaiming himself the Messiah. The various New Testament accounts place the blame for most of what followed squarely on the Jews. Many of them were outraged at Jesus' claim; they saw it as a blasphemous statement, particularly those belonging to the religious factions, the Pharisees and Zealots.

As a result Jesus was arrested and taken before the High Priest Caiaphas, a Pharisee, who agreed that Christ had committed blasphemy. Caiaphas ordered him to appear before Roman Governor Pontius Pilate for punishment. According to Matthew's gospel, Pilate asked Jesus: "Art Thou the King of the Jews?" Jesus responded with an ambiguous: "Thou sayest."[2] Although it was not a denial, Pilate attempted to have Jesus released because he did not believe he had done anything to deserve execution. However, *"When Pilate saw that he could prevail nothing, but that rather a tumult was made, he took water, and washed his hands before the multitude, saying, I am innocent of the blood of this just person: see ye to it."*[3] Jesus was then taken to a place outside Jerusalem (Calvary) and crucified along with two other men, accused robbers.

The gospels vary on the date of the Crucifixion. According to John, it took place on the eve of the Sabbath.[4] As it was against Jewish law for those crucified to remain on the cross on the Sabbath, the Jews asked Pilate for permission to break the legs of Jesus and the other two to ensure they were dead, thus enabling their bodies to be removed.[5] It is at this point we find the first mention of what has become the legend of the Holy Lance.

"But when they came to Jesus, and saw that he was dead already, they brake not his legs: But one of the soldiers with a spear pierced his side, and forthwith came there out blood and water. And he that saw it bare record, and his record is true: and he knoweth that he saith true, that ye might believe. For these things were done, that the Scripture should be fulfilled. A bone of him shall not be broken. And again another Scripture saith, They shall look on him whom they have pierced."[6]

It is accepted among many religious scholars that the scriptures mentioned here are a reference to the Old Testament. This poses the question: Did the story of the Holy Lance have its origins in that part of the Bible? If Jesus was pierced with a lance it could be argued that it was the fulfillment of a prophecy of Zechariah: *"and they shall look upon me whom they have pierced, and they shall mourn for him, as one mourneth for his only son, and shall be in bitterness for him, as one that is in bitterness for his first born."*[7]

The subject of this piercing is made clear by Zechariah when he speaks of the prophecy of the Messiah's triumphal arrival in Jerusalem: *"Behold the King cometh unto thee; he is just and having salvation; lowly, and riding upon an ass."*[8] Another passage reads: *"And one shall say unto him, What are those wounds in thine hands? Then he shall answer, Those with which I was wounded in the house of my friends."*[9] The Hebrew translation of Zechariah differs slightly: *"And they shall look unto Me because they have thrust him through."*[10]

The latter reference is still undeniably to a Messiah. The difference in translation has to do with the Jewish belief in the coming of two Messiahs. In the text of Zechariah the first Messiah is prophesying the fate of the second. The Christian belief is in the one Messiah who has already come and will return.

Further, the apostle John's phrase "a bone of him shall not be broken" is attributed by some writers to Isaiah's prophecy of the coming Messiah.[11] Many Christians believe that the fact that Jesus' body was spared from mutilation signified that he was the Messiah. However, questions arise: Did the Jewish soldiers intend to kill Christ with Herod's lance, which they allegedly took with them to the cross as their symbol of authority,[12] thereby fulfilling, deliberately or otherwise, an Old Testament prophecy of the fate of one of their Messiahs? Was the prophecy fulfilled by a Roman soldier, knowingly or otherwise (in this context it does not matter) by the act of piercing Jesus' body?

The veracity of both stories is very much open to question as is the hypothesis that the essential lines of the Lance legend (*But one of the soldiers with a spear pierced his side, and forthwith came there out blood and water*[13]) were inserted by early church leaders at some later date along with other material!*

There is more to the biblical implications of this story. Ronald Aharon, a New York State University Jewish scholar who has made a study of law, martyrdom, and deliverance in early rabbinic religiosity, argues that the way in which a messiah dies is important to what he calls the advent of messianic deliverance. "It is not 'merely' his suffering and death but the fact that he stands heroically

---

*In their book *The Holy Blood and the Holy Grail* (London: Corgi, 1982), authors Michael Baigent, Richard Leigh, and Henry Lincoln assert that on the basis of their research John's gospel "had been subjected to doctoring, editing, expurgating, and revision" (p. 346).

in 'battle' where it is *clear beforehand* that death *must* be the result. In other words, his death is a martyrdom, not a vicarious martyrdom . . . but a heroic death suffered by the messiah. . . ."[14]

Aharon is not, of course, discussing Christ's death, but his words summarize the widely accepted Christian view of the martyrdom of Christ: his almost certain execution as a result of proclaiming himself the Messiah after riding into Jerusalem, and then not denying it to Pilate. Here was a man who stood heroically in battle—if only a battle for the hearts and minds—which he must have known he would lose; his martyrdom was real enough.

Aharon quotes the great sage Rabbi Eliezer ben Hyrcanus as saying that without martyrdom deliverance cannot penetrate into the dimension of the present.[15] Were similar observations, by coincidence, made by the early Church when it came to write the story of the Crucifixion? For it could be argued that the thrust of the lance into Christ's side provided not only the fulfillment of a prophecy regarding the true Messiah but the emphasis that has propelled the story of deliverance through Jesus to this day!

However, Dr. Barbara Thiering, author of the international bestseller *Jesus the Man,* brings us back to reality: "To say the Old Testament is predicting is to impose on it an unnatural view. The Old Testament made sense in its own time." In other words, it was written for its time and not as a document of prophecy.

As we have seen in the previous chapter, Ravenscroft names as the soldier who allegedly wielded the lance veteran Roman centurion Gauis Cassius who was at the Crucifixion as the representative of Pilate.[16] Cassius was upset and angered at the dreadful mutilations of the two robbers crucified by the guards from the Jewish temple. The guards had crushed their skulls as well as broken their limbs to ensure death. At the same time Cassius, like Pilate, was also touched by Christ's serene manner.[17]

To prevent Christ's body being similarly mutilated, Cassius charged his horse toward the cross and thrust the lance into Jesus' right side, between the fourth and fifth ribs. This was a ritual method used by Roman soldiers following a battle to ensure its fallen enemies were actually dead, or as a *coup de grace*.[18] It would appear that this was a difficult feat for Cassius: Ravenscroft tells us he had cataracts in both eyes and could barely see—until the moment the lance entered Christ's body at which time Cassius' failing sight was miraculously restored.[19]

Shortly after his resurrection Jesus appeared before Mary Magdalene and at another meeting before eleven of his twelve disciples.[20] Thomas, the absent disciple, when told of the appearances said he would not believe Jesus had come back from the dead until he could see and touch his wounds. As a result we find another mention, also brief, of the wounding of Jesus' side. Jesus appeared before Doubting Thomas and asked him to examine the wounds made by the nails and the Lance. "Reach hither thy finger, and behold my hands; and reach hither thy hand, and thrust it into my side."[21]

According to Dr. Thiering, John's gospel is "not an invention of the Crucifixion": it is a down-to-earth retelling by an eyewitness of events the way they occurred. John was the only one of those whose names are given to the gospels who was there as the events unfolded. *"He* [John] *that saw it bare record, and his record is true; and he knoweth that he saith true, that ye might believe."*[22]

As for the dating of John, Thiering said it was the first of the gospels to be written, completed by A.D. 37. Its writer was Philip the evangelist "contrary to scholarly opinion."[23] Philip was also known as "the centurion's servant,"[24] which would appear to link him even more closely to John.

The centurion could not have been Ravenscroft's Cassius,[25] according to Dr. Thiering's findings. The centurion was, in fact, John himself: John pierced the side of Christ. John was also a Roman centurion, whose given name was Eutychus. In addition, he was a close friend of Jesus. In fact, most of the early gentile followers were from among the Roman soldiers stationed in Jerusalem at the time.

Dr. Thiering went on to say that John was a centurion in another sense in that he was head of a group of one hundred gentile initiates who were converts to the new religion and had modeled their community on one of the Jewish factions, the Essenes.

John had medical knowledge and was doing something that is a standard test for life in use to this day. "An important sign is that if a cut be made in the skin or a vessel be opened no bleeding takes place after death."[26] Therefore, when the blood flowed from Jesus' side from the cut made by John, he knew that Jesus almost certainly was alive.

Further mention of a centurion at the Crucifixion is found in Mark's gospel. The first occurs when Jesus on the cross "gave up the ghost" (spirit): an unnamed centurion "which stood over against him . . . said, Truly this man was the Son of God."[27]

Later, Pilate, marvelling at the news that Jesus had died so quickly, turns for confirmation of the death to this anonymous centurion, and "when he knew it of the centurion" Pilate gave Jesus' body to Joseph of Arimathea.[28] The "Son of God" comment would fit the image of John as would his confirming to Pilate that Jesus was dead: If the centurion in question was John and he had carried out the test for a sign of life, then he was lying to Pilate!

Jesus, according to Thiering, was not dead, nor had he been drugged. The vinegar wine he had been offered and which he drank just before dying had, in fact, been poisoned.[29] It was, therefore a matter of crucial timing whether Jesus lived or died. If we accept the vital role of the centurion in this story, then, had Pilate not believed him when he asked the soldier "whether he had been any while dead,"[30] the history of the world might well have been different. Obviously, before the poison took effect Jesus had to be quickly removed from the cross so that he could be revived.

According to Thiering, this was done. Jesus was immediately placed in a sepulchre (a burial place—in this case, a cave). A vessel containing a very large amount of myrrh and aloes was left beside him. Aloe juice acts as a purgative and in large quantities acts quickly while the myrrh is a soothing ingredient. Together these helped revive Jesus.[31] "John's gospel is giving us the facts as clearly as can be," Thiering insisted in an interview with me.

Dr. Thiering's comments and findings, when applied to the

story of the Holy Lance, help us put the legend into perspective. However, even if we accept all of her compelling evidence that there was no supernatural involvement in this and other aspects of the Crucifixion, it does not mean that we can dismiss the legend of the Holy Lance as such. We must deal with its myth which is in circulation to this day. The legend in the present context seeks to cast an aura upon Adolf Hitler, another man of history who was also all too human and the antithesis of all that Jesus stood for.

Notes

1. Quoted in Antonia Fraser, *Cromwell: Our Chief of Men* (London: Weidenfeld & Nicolson, 1973), p. 39.
2. Matthew 27:11 KJV.
3. Matthew 27:24.
4. John 19:14.
5. John 19:31.
6. John 19:33–37.
7. Zechariah 12:10.
8. Zechariah 9:9.
9. Zechariah 13:6:
10. Cited by Aharon E. Agus, *The Binding of Isaac and Messiah* (Albany: State University of New York Press, 1988), p. 207.
11. See, for example, Trevor Ravenscroft, *The Spear of Destiny* (York Beach, Me.: Samuel Weiser Inc., 1982), p. ix.
12. Ibid., p. x.
13. John 19:33–37.
14. Aharon, *The Binding of Isaac and Messiah,* p. 209, n. 5.
15. Ibid., p. 211.
16. Ravenscroft, *The Spear of Destiny,* pp. x–xi.
17. Ibid., p. xi.
18. Ibid.
19. Ibid.
20. Mark 16:16.
21. John 20:27.
22. John 19:35.

23. Barbara Thiering, *Jesus the Man* (New York: Bantam Doubleday, 1992), p. 102.

24. Ibid., p. 547.

25. Ravenscroft, *The Spear of Destiny*, p. ix.

26. *Black's Medical Dictionary* (London: A & C Black, 1955), p. 235.

27. Mark 15:39.

28. Mark 15:45.

29. Thiering, *Jesus the Man*, p. 183, n. 2.

30. John 15:44.

31. Thiering, *Jesus the Man*, p. 160.

5

Doubtful Sources

Ravenscroft tells us that at the end of his research into the history of the Holy Lance Hitler returned to the museum and stood once again before it. He then entered into a trance state. "I slowly became aware of a mighty presence around it, the same awesome presence which I had experienced inwardly on those rare occasions in my life when I had sensed that a great destiny awaited me. . . . A window in the future was opened up to me through which I saw in a single flash of illumination a future event by which I knew beyond contradiction that the blood in my veins would one day become the vessel of the Folk-Spirit of my people.[1]

"The aura became stifling so that I could hardly breathe. The noisy scene of the Treasure House (Hapsburg Museum) seemed to melt away before my eyes. I stood alone and trembling before the hovering form of the Superman (*Ubermensch*)—a spirit sublime and fearful, a countenance *intrepid and cruel*. I offered my soul as a vessel of his will."[2]

Hitler, it seems, has somehow transmogrified the spirit of the Holy Lance into the mythologized Aryan Superman.

Ravenscroft goes on to say that Hitler described the same vision he had in the museum to Hermann Rauschning, the Nazi Gauleiter we met in chapter 3, who fled from Germany before World War II. As noted in that chapter, Rauschning claimed he had recorded his conversations with Hitler. The description came up in a conversation in which the two were discussing the mutation of the German race. Ravenscroft gives as evidence the following passage which he cites as an extract from Rauschning's 1939 book *Hitler Speaks*:

> "The Superman is living amongst us now! He is here!" exclaimed Hitler triumphantly. "Isn't that enough for you? I have seen the New Man. He is *intrepid and cruel.* I was afraid of him." In uttering these words, Hitler was trembling in a kind of ecstasy.[3]

At best it is flimsy supporting evidence for Ravenscroft's assertion. There are other points to be made about this. We know Rauschning spoke to Hitler a number of times, whereas there is no objective record that Ravenscroft's mentor, Stein, the source of these quotes, spoke to Hitler at all. Second, the passages referring to the Superman in both quotes have a similar ring to them, although they must have been uttered twenty years apart, Ravenscroft's passage being the first in chronological order. Finally, and perhaps coincidentally, in both quotes used by Ravenscroft the phrase *intrepid and cruel* appears, although, as we shall see, it does not appear in the original English translation of the same passage. The one that we must accept is cited by Ravenscroft.

Ravenscroft makes the controversial statement that Rauschning is "surely the only authentic biographer of Adolf Hitler."[4] This is another claim that weakens under objective examination. The Rauschning material is used by researchers and historians, both orthodox and occult, as a source of information on Hitler for a short period of his life in the early thirties. It can hardly be said to provide a detailed biography of Hitler the man. The German historian Theodore Schieder, for example, finds Rauschning's material to be of unquestionable value *for this period* since it contains views derived from immediate experience and is the testimony of an intelligent witness.[5] However, the controversial British historian David Irving is quite dismissive of Rauschning, the former Danzig politician who was for some time a staunch supporter of Hitler. Irving complains that Rauschning's oft-quoted book published in 1939 has bedeviled analyses of Hitler's policies ever since. He argues that an internal Nazi investigation showed that Rauschning met Hitler only a couple of times on formal occasions.[6] Irving does not enlarge on this claim, but it is obvious the Nazis would have wanted to play down any close relationship between the two men given the nature of the material in question and its propaganda potential at the time of publication.

Schieder estimates that Rauschning met with Hitler, at most, thirteen times, and was alone with him during about six of these meetings[7]—enough time for any reasonably astute observer to have formed some idea of the character and thoughts of a person.

Irving goes on to cite a chapter which he says was deleted from the original edition (1939) of Rauschning's book *Hitler Speaks,* but was included in the 1973 edition published in Vienna. This chapter, he finds, "is revealing in more senses than one, as it purported to describe how Hitler regularly woke up at night screaming 'It's Him—Him,' meaning the devil." This "disposes of Rauschning's credibility once and for all."[8]

Irving may well see this extract as solid evidence against Rauschning, but his promotion of it creates some confusion. The passage to which he appears to be referring was certainly not deleted from the 1939 British edition of *Hitler Speaks.* Its use does not, incidentally, appear to have damaged Rauschning's credibility as such.

Our main interest is the alleged occult implications implied in the material in question: Hitler feared he had been visited by the Devil. Therefore it is necessary and enlightening to look at the material in context.

Whatever is said about it is certainly not complimentary to Hitler. Rauschning wrote:

Hitler, however, has states that approach persecution mania and dual personality. His sleeplessness is more than the mere result of excessive nervous strain. He often wakes in the middle of the night and wanders restlessly to and fro. Then he must have light everywhere. Lately he has sent at these times for young men who have to keep him company during his hours of manifest anguish. At times these conditions must have become dreadful. A man in the closest daily association with him gave me this account: "Hitler wakes at night with convulsive shrieks. He shouts for help. He sits on the edge of his bed, as if unable to stir. He shakes with fear, making the whole bed vibrate. He shouts confused, totally unintelligible phrases. He gasps, as if imagining himself to be suffocating."

My informant described to me in full details a remarkable scene—I should not have credited the story if it had not come from such a source. Hitler stood swaying in his room looking wildly about him. "He! He! He's been here!" he gasped. His lips were blue. Sweat streamed down his face. Suddenly he began to reel off figures, and odd words and broken phrases, entirely devoid of sense. It sounded horrible. He used strangely composed and entirely un-German word-formations. Then he stood quite still, only his lips moving. He was massaged and offered something to drink. Then he suddenly broke out—"There, there! In the corner! Who's that?"

He stamped and shrieked in the familiar way. He was shown that there was nothing out of the ordinary in the room and then he gradually grew calm. After that he lay asleep for many hours.[9]

Apart from the fact that the passage was not omitted from the original edition of the book, as Irving asserts, there are several other points to be made. The first is that Rauschning is not relating a first-person account. Second, Rauschning does not write, as Irving claims, that Hitler "regularly woke up at night screaming 'It's Him— Him.' " The circumstance in which this phrase arose refers to a particular incident, although Hitler's "night terrors" were obviously not unusual. Finally, Rauschning does not claim Hitler meant the Devil when he screamed in terror, "He! He! He's been here." In fact, Rauschning does not speculate on who the being or entity may have been—if any.

This comment of Hitler's recorded by Rauschning offers us one theory as to who this terrifying vision was.* Note it differs from the passage Ravenscroft assigns to Rauschning. Further, it

---

*The source is the original translation of Rauschning's book.

does not say "Hitler was trembling in a kind of ecstasy as he uttered the words"—a "literary device" of Ravenscroft?

> The new man is among us! He is here! . . . I will tell you a secret. I have seen the vision of the new man—fearless and formidable. I shrank from him.[10]

Hitler's nemesis was the Superman! It is worth repeating that Rauschning does not speculate on this startling statement.

Miller has her own idea as to the identity of the mysterious visitor who so upset Hitler that night: not the Devil, not the Superman or even some apparition from Hitler's alleged occult connections. The being was his father! "No one grasped the connection between his panic and the senseless numbers he was mouthing that night. The feelings of fear he had repressed in his childhood when counting his father's blows (as he hit Hitler) now overtook the adult at the peak of his success in the form of nightmares, sudden and inescapable."[11]

Joachim Fest is not as dismissive of Rauschning as Irving. He finds authenticity in the conversations. They "have preserved something of the self-important intonation of a man wonderstruck by his own tirades," Fest writes.[12] Schwaab fulsomely finds that Rauschning was one of those rare, perceptive writers of the time who not only urgently, early, and correctly forewarned the Free World of the dangers Hitler posed, but also plainly showed that Hitler was "not normal." However, Schwaab is as cautious of Hitler's dialogues as we must be of Ravenscroft.[13]

Undaunted, Ravenscroft pushes on, claiming a striking similarity between Rauschning's descriptions of Hitler and passages about Landulf of Capua "from the manuscripts of the medieval Chronicler Echempertus."[14]

According to Ravenscroft, Hitler claimed he was the reincarnation of Landulf, the character on which Richard Wagner's Klingsor is supposedly based in his *Parsifal*.[15] Klingsor is also the ninth-century black magician in the Grail legends. Landulf, like Hitler, used the swastika as his heraldic device.[16] "By comparing the two sets of documents separated by a thousand years, one is struck by the resemblance in the characters, lives, and attitudes of the German Führer and the medieval Klingsor," enthuses Ravenscroft.[17]

British occult author Michael FitzGerald offers a possible source of such claims which have led to Hitler's reputation as an expert in the occult and an initiate of secret societies, privy to esoteric and ancient knowledge—in short, a man with the powers to decipher the mysteries of the Holy Lance. A Martha Kunzel repeatedly and unsuccessfully urged Hitler to adopt *The Book of Law,* written by the infamous British magician and occultist Aleister Crowley. One reason for her failure to convince Hitler was that he wanted *Mein Kampf* to be the only "holy book" in Germany. "And yet," FitzGerald goes on, "there are so many striking sentences in Rauschning's account where Hitler is—often word for word—paraphrasing or expressing an idea from *The Book of Law.*"[18]

This raises the question not asked by FitzGerald: Did Rauschning use Crowley's book as an inspiration or source, or did he even plagiarize when he wrote *Hitler Speaks* years later and without notes? The suspicion that he did all three must remain, especially as we have seen that Ravenscroft finds that Rauschning's descriptions of Hitler and passages about Landulf of Capua also bear a striking similarity. Was the medieval Chronicler Echempertus another source from which Rauschning drew to put words into Hitler's mouth?

Rauschning on one occasion sarcastically described Nazism as "the St. Vitus Dance of the twentieth century." He regarded Hitler as completely unprincipled, an opportunist who respected nothing, believed in nothing, feared nothing, and broke the most solemn oaths without a qualm.[19] Given such a view, it would not come as a surprise to learn that Rauschning had treated his subject with contempt and filled his mouth with esoteric drivel that has since become resource material for both occult and orthodox researchers.

Notes

1. Trevor Ravenscroft, *The Spear of Destiny* (York Beach, Me.: Samuel Weiser Inc., 1982), p. 20.

2. Ibid., p. 38.

3. Ibid.

4. Ibid., p. 175.

5. German historian Theodore Schieder in Otto Wagener, *Hitler: Memoirs of a Confidant,* ed. Henry Ashby Turner, trans. Ruth Hein (New Haven, Conn.: Yale University Press, 1985), pp. xv–xvi.

6. David Irving, *The War Path* (London: Michael Joseph, 1978), p. x.

7. Wagener, *Hitler: Memoirs of a Confidant,* p. xvi, n. 5.

8. Irving, *The War Path,* p. x.

9. Hermann Rauschning, *Hitler Speaks* (London: Butterworth, 1939), pp. 250–51.

10. Ibid., p. 245.

11. Alice Miller, *For Your Own Good* (London: Virago Press, 1987), p. 174.

12. Joachim C. Fest, *Hitler* (Hammondsworth, Middlesex, U.K.: Pelican Books edition, 1977), p. 775.

13. Edleff Schwaab, *Hitler's Mind: A Plunge into Madness* (New York: Praeger, 1992), p. 17.

14. Ravenscroft, *The Spear of Destiny,* p. 175, n. 1.

15. Ibid., p. 88.

16. Michael FitzGerald, *Storm Troopers of Satan* (London: Robert Hale, 1990), p. 109.

17. Ravenscroft, *The Spear of Destiny,* p. 178.

18. FitzGerald, *Storm Troopers of Satan,* p. 174, n. 16.

19. Fest, *Hitler,* p. 306, n. 12.

6

The Undergraduate Meets Hitler

Who was Ravenscroft's mentor, Walter Johannes Stein? Ravenscroft tells us that, like Hitler, Stein was an Austrian and only a year or so younger than the Führer. Born in Vienna in 1891, Stein was the second son of a well-to-do family of attorneys who were specialists in international law. Although he graduated in science, he wrote his doctoral dissertation on philosophy. He was also an expert in medieval and ancient art and a pupil and associate of Rudolf Steiner[1] (1861-1925), an Austrian philosopher and educator who also founded anthroposophy, an awkward sounding word meaning literally "wisdom about man." Steiner claimed the source of his teachings was "spiritual research" based on an exact scientific mode of supersensible perception. A central thesis of anthroposophy is that humanity's present intellectual capacities have evolved from a more primitive consciousness. An essential task for humanity today is to carry the clarity and objectivity of the improved intellect into new modes of spiritual perception. Steiner saw this being done through the use of imagination, inspiration, and intuition. Such a "resurrection" of consciousness has become possible, Steiner held, through Christ uniting himself with the destiny of humankind on earth.[2] More simply, the occult writer Colin Wilson summarizes anthroposophy as the most comprehensive of all occult systems.[3] It is a recognition that there is a world beyond the material world revealed by our senses, a

view held by mystics such as William Blake. Wilson argues that
Steiner in his writings—like Blake—could actually see or catch
glimpses of this "supersensible" world.[4] It is apparent from the
words Ravenscroft ascribes to Hitler that Ravenscroft would have
us believe Hitler, in his encounters with the Holy Lance and the
frightening figure of a Superman, caught glimpses of this "world
beyond" through similar supersensual experiences.[5]

Ravenscroft even claims that Steiner, too, had stood transfixed
before the Holy Lance, as an eighteen-year-old science student
at Vienna University in 1879, exactly thirty years before Hitler
had seen the lance. Steiner had found in the experience inspiration
to help humankind, whereas Hitler was to find only evil.[6] Ravenscroft tells a story of Steiner and Hitler that amounts to a
battle for survival between two occult forces. In the twenties Hitler
came to regard Steiner as his greatest enemy ranting against him
at political meetings and accusing him of using magic to influence
the minds of German leaders. Ravenscroft claims Steiner had
discovered the satanic nature of the Thule Society. Among the
pre-World War I members of this racist group were occultists.
However, post-war the society emerged as a powerful right-wing,
nationalistic force within the upper echelon of Bavarian society.
In the Communist uprising of 1919 it is said to have organized
a terrorist network which supplied arms to the rightist forces and
distributed German nationalist and anti-Semitic literature. Its
members started the German Workers party which Hitler turned
into the Nazi party. (See chapter 11 for further details.[7]) Steiner
was openly engaged in warning Germany of the secret aims of
the Nazis and had been put at the top of the Thule's assassination
list.[8] In 1922 Walter Stein, who had infiltrated the Thulists, heard
they planned to assassinate Steiner inside a railway carriage at
Munich station: he was to be blasted in the face at close range
with a sawed-off shotgun. The plot was foiled by the timely arrival
at the station of Stein with some of his associates. After being
rescued, Steiner fled Germany for Switzerland.[9]

Steiner was lecturing in those post-World War I years in
Germany at the same time Hitler was "lecturing" his way to fame,

but their messages were very different. Steiner was encouraging people to think on a higher plane of consciousness, while Hitler's preaching was basic race hatred and virulent nationalism, a thoroughly low-consciousness level of thinking with consequent mass appeal.

The fact remains, at this time the fledgling Nazis were too concerned about destroying the powerful Communists to worry about relative weaklings who were preaching utopian ideals. Wilson says Steiner (rather than being the main enemy to the Nazis) "was simply an irrelevance."[10] However, he did attract flak on one occasion when he chose to preach against patriotism in Hitler's new hometown, Munich, the birthplace of the Nazis. During a lecture in Munich in May 1922, young Nazis continually interrupted Steiner. Later in the city's Four Seasons Hotel, he was physically attacked and only the prompt intervention of his friends saved him from injury. Escaping through a back door, he decided that for the time being things were too dangerous for him in Germany.[11]

Thus we have two very different accounts of what is obviously the same incident: one an alleged planned assassination attempt in the confined space of a railway carriage, the other a "roughing up" by thugs, to intimidate only, in the comparatively public space of a hotel.

There is one other matter in which the accounts of Ravenscroft and Wilson are at variance relative to the story of Steiner and Hitler. Dr. Steiner had built a temple called Goetheanum in the foothills of the Jura Mountains, in Switzerland, circa 1920. According to Ravenscroft, it was the greatest wish of Dietrich Eckart (a crony of Hitler and the spiritual founder of the Nazis, claimed by some to have been a leading member of the Thule Society[12]) that it be burnt to the ground and that Steiner and his immediate circle of disciples should die in flames. On New Year's Eve 1923, while Dr. Steiner was giving a lecture before some eight hundred people, the building was torched. The fire had not been discovered until after the audience had left. A German-Swiss watchmaker and fanatical Nazi (who Ravenscroft does not name) had set the fire. His charred body was found in the ruins. His payment for the evil deed, gold coins, was laying beside him.[13] A less dramatic interpretation comes from Wilson who places the fire a year earlier, New Year's Eve 1922. Once again a less dramatic reality intrudes: The fact that the fire began inside a wall of the building suggests an electrical fault.[14]

Ravenscroft relates that Walter Stein, as a student in pre-World War I Vienna, came to meet Hitler while pursuing his own investigations into the *Parsifal* legend as part of his German literature studies. One day Stein found in a grubby little bookshop a copy of Wolfram von Eschenbach's *Parsifal,* which had been heavily annotated. Intrigued, he bought it.[15] Later, glancing through the book at a café, he concluded that the notes showed their writer to have a deep knowledge of the occult, that he had delved into black magic, and that he was an avid racist.[16] This was a rather presumptive judgment if, in fact, Stein had just begun studying the subject.

As Stein read on, feeling both impressed and disgusted, he felt compelled to look up: he did so, into the eyes of a shabbily dressed man holding three postcard size paintings outside the café window. The man wore a tiny beard and moustache and was obviously trying to sell the paintings to passersby. Their eyes met and Stein felt as though he were being hypnotized. He left the café and found himself buying all three paintings.[17]

Back at home, Stein glanced at the water colorings for the first time. One depicted the Holy Lance. But what intrigued him was the signature on each—Adolf Hitler, the same name as on the annotated book he had bought that same day![18]

Stein returned to the bookshop hoping to track down Hitler. Its owner, Herr Ernst Pretzsche, showed him other books in which Hitler had scribbled. Pretzsche said Hitler pawned the books to enable him to buy food. He redeemed them when he could afford to by selling his paintings. *Parsifal* had been sold to Stein by mistake.

The other books included works of Georg Hegel, Friedrich Nietzsche, Johann Fichte, Friedrich Schelling, and Houston S. Chamberlain's *Foundations of the Nineteenth Century,* written, its author said, under the influence of demons.[19] Chamberlain's racist tract can be summarized as arguing that the superior mental powers of the German must guide the Aryan peoples to supremacy and world domination.[20] Other books were on mythology, oriental religions, and yoga.[21]

Pretzsche told Stein that he himself was an authority on the occult and had initiated Hitler into the art of black magic and the secrets hidden behind astrological and alchemical symbolism.[22]

When Stein did meet Hitler they had long discussions in which Stein found himself struggling against Hitler's compelling attempts to convert him to a belief in the superiority of the German race. Stein for his part, recognizing Hitler's exceptional gifts of hypnotic persuasion, tried unsuccessfully to arouse in Hitler some compassion for the rest of humanity.[23]

One day Stein and Hitler visited together the Holy Lance in its museum showcase. Gazing at it the undergraduate felt himself transported into a state of ecstasy; a deep feeling of love and healing seemed to come from it. However, when he looked at Hitler, his feelings changed abruptly. Hitler stood swaying back and forth, mesmerized. Suddenly Stein felt he was looking at the anti-Christ, the reincarnation of Landulf the practitioner of black magic, sexual perversions, and human sacrifice.[24]

Stein had come across Landulf in his own research and what he had found was horrifying. Landulf had practiced the most appalling rites of black magic, involving not only sexual perversions, but human sacrifice.[25] These rites were used to initiate Hitler into his final pact with the powers of darkness.[26]

Shortly after their outing to the museum, Ravenscroft concludes, the two men parted company for the last time.[27]

It is important for the veracity of Ravenscroft's account of Stein's meetings with Hitler that the closeness of the two men at that time be established. Ravenscroft makes it clear that the relationship could never be described as a friendship. However, as any psychologist dealing with patients will testify, friendship is not necessary for a relationship to be structured, deliberately or otherwise, between two people in such a manner that it leads to understanding and empathy and finally disclosure of thoughts, feelings, and beliefs. Was the Stein-Hitler relationship structured, even part of the way, along these lines?

Ravenscroft supplies some clues. For example, he says that Hitler in their meetings never used Stein's first name. Nor did he ever use the intimate form of "Du." Instead, he sarcastically called the young student "Herr Professor" or "Herr Doktor." Further, the onus was always on Stein to arrange their meetings. "On many occasions" Hitler did not keep appointments and Stein had to go looking for him in his customary haunts. Hitler was also moody, some days willing to speak "very openly about certain aspects of his occult experiences" while at other times he confined his conversations to tedious political or racial diatribes.[28]

None of this gives the impression that Hitler and Stein were at all close. It is safe to assume that no empathy leading to inti- mate, willing, and open disclosure developed. In fact, Hitler's later close cronies complained that one of the worst things about Hitler was that you never knew what he was thinking. "Who can boast knowing another human being when that person had not opened up to him the most hidden corners of his mind," said Alfred Jodl when speaking of Hitler at the Nuremberg War Trials in 1945. The chief of staff of the Wehrmacht High Command, who was at Hitler's side every day for years, went on: "I do not even know to this day what *he* thought, knew, and wanted to do, but rather what I thought and suspected about it."[29]

"If Hitler had any friends I would certainly have been one of his closest," says Albert Speer, who spent an endless amount of time with Hitler in his inner circle and was, moreover, his favored associate in one of the subjects that most interested him, archi- tecture. Speer goes on to admit that "never in my life had I met a person who so seldom revealed his feelings and if he did, instantly locked them away."[30] He had agreed with Hitler's deputy, Rudolf Hess, that there had been moments when the two men felt they had come close to Hitler, "but we were . . . inevitably disillusioned. If either one of us ventured a slightly personal tone, Hitler promptly put up an unbreakable wall."

Yet it is Ravenscroft's assertion that Stein came close to Hitler and was moved enough to have some compassion for him.[31] Was Stein one of the very few who Hitler did allow into the private world of his thoughts and feelings? If so, why? For what purpose? Why was Stein so uniquely chosen?

Getting back to the encounters between the two men, Ravenscroft says they took place in the late summer, autumn, and winter of 1912 and in the spring of 1913.[32] When Stein first met Hitler, one of Hitler's aunts had recently died and left him a small legacy, as a result of which his status had greatly improved, including his appearance from the day that Stein had first set eyes on him from the coffee shop. Stein found a neat and tidy man, hair barbered, dressed in a new suit, white shirt, and shiny boots.[33]

FitzGerald casts doubts on these dates and in doing so he shows a fault in the memory processes of either Stein or Ravenscroft, or both. Hitler's aunt died in March 1911, the spring of that year, not the summer of the following year.[34] Any conversations must have taken place between 1911 and 1912. Further, Hitler was lying when he told Stein he was going to Munich. Hitler went to Liverpool (England) in 1912. He stayed with his sister-in-law's family "for some time."[35]

Incidentally, FitzGerald also says that while in Vienna Hitler had been constantly moving from one cheap rooming house to another for some years to avoid conscription in the Austrian army. (It wasn't because he was so impecunious that he could not afford to pay for his lodgings and so kept being evicted?*)

Paradoxically, despite the contradictions FitzGerald raises, he largely relies on Ravenscroft as the source for his material on the Holy Lance.

Ravenscroft says that Stein was a strong anti-Nazi who fled to Britain. During World War II he worked as a British intelligence agent bringing back from the Continent the plans for the German invasion of Britain, "Operation Sea Lion."[36] Stein was also wartime confidential adviser to Sir Winston Churchill on the

---

*There does not appear to be much substance in the story that Hitler was avoiding military service. When war broke out in 1914, Hitler was in Munich. He rushed to volunteer for the German army and was overjoyed when accepted.

"minds and motivation of Adolf Hitler and the leading members of his party."[37]

Stein's wartime activity is cited by Ravenscroft as an important reason why *The Spear of Destiny* was not written until after he had died. Very considerable pressure was brought to bear to dissuade Stein. Churchill was most insistent that the occultism of the Nazi party "should not under any circumstances be revealed to the general public" in the years immediately following the war.[38] Stein understood the rationale behind this was an agreement made "at the highest levels" to explain the atrocious crimes of the Nazis as the result of mental aberration and the systematic perversion of instincts, rather than have to reveal that such practices were an integral part of a dedicated service to evil occultic powers.[39]

In any case, Stein believed that another three decades would have to pass before there would be enough people to comprehend the initiation rites and black magic practices of the inner core of the Nazi leadership.[40] However, the publication of Aldous Huxley's *The Doors of Perception* in 1957 convinced Stein otherwise: public opinion had changed sufficiently for him to publish his own work on the legend of the lance and its influence on Hitler. Among other things, Huxley's book attacks what he saw as the prevailing skepticism toward occultism and the existence of higher levels of consciousness.[41]

With the obstacles at last removed to revealing what on the surface was one of the most sensational accounts of Hitler and Nazi Germany, Stein suddenly died. Ravenscroft gives us only the barest details of his sudden passing: It happened three days after Stein's decision to publish. He collapsed in the study of his London home and died in a hospital soon afterward. Ravenscroft realized it was up to him to write the book.[42]

Among the first areas he had to research was the history of the lance. Let us look independently at that history. Doing so helps us judge the accuracy of the picture painted by Ravenscroft and other tellers of the story of Hitler's alleged association with the holy object.

The first known record of the existence of a lance in physical form occurs in the sixth century when the pilgrim St. Antoninus of Piacenza says he saw it in the Mount Zion basilica in Jerusalem,[43] centuries after it was supposedly used to pierce Christ's side. Why did it suddenly reappear?

Ruth Lewin-Broit, a religious studies scholar, speculates that one reason may be that the sixth-century church leaders were working on how to make Christianity into a fighting religion. The symbolic value of a weapon of war that also had sacred connotations would have been of definite appeal, just as the story of the centurion and the lance could have been used in the campaign to convert the Romans in earlier times.

Another early record says that with the capture of Jerusalem by the Persians in 615 C.E. the shaft of the lance fell into the hands of the pagans, together with the other relics of the Crucifixion.[44] Its point, which had been broken off, was saved and given to Nicetas, who brought it to Constantinople where it was kept in Santa Sophia Church set in an icon. In 1241 it was given to French King Louis and preserved in the Sainte-Chapelle in Paris together with the Crown of Thorns. The lance head disappeared during the French Revolution.[45] Another account says emphatically that this lance was destroyed during that revolution.[46]

The other part of the lance was said to have been sent to Jerusalem by the Frankish pilgrim Arculf (ca. 670). After that nothing is heard of it until it reappears in Constantinople before the tenth century. In 1492 it fell into the hands of the Turks who sent it to the pope as a present. Since then it has been kept in Rome under the dome of St. Peter's, but its authenticity has always been doubted.[47]

Archeological evidence has shown conclusively the lance first mentioned in the sixth century is not the one in the Hapsburg Museum in Vienna. The museum lance is known as the Lance of St. Maurice, or Constantine's Lance, which did not exist before the eighth or ninth century[48] and appears to have disappeared from history for the next few hundred years.

The *New Catholic Encyclopedia* says there is evidence of the history of the Maurice Lance since the tenth century.[49] It was used as a symbol of the imperial power bestowed upon the Holy Roman emperors at the time of their coronation.[50] However, *The Oxford Dictionary of the Christian Church,* noting that the Maurice Lance is one of several relics claimed to be the Holy Lance, would appear to give it a somewhat less exalted status. It says simply that it was one of the objects "kept among the imperial insignia of the Holy Roman Empire."[51] It was first noted in Prague around 1350, then in Nuremberg in 1424, where it stayed until it was taken to Vienna in 1800.[52]

Both the Oxford dictionary and the *New Catholic Encyclopedia* note yet another claimant, discovered during the First Crusade at Antioch in 1098. This lance was in the possession of Raymond IV of Toulouse until 1101 when it was lost during a battle in Asia Minor. From the early thirteenth century the Armenians have had a holy lance whose origins are unknown. "It may be significant that this lance appeared in Armenia not long after the Antioch lance was lost, but it is impossible to prove that the two lances are identical," notes the *New Catholic Encyclopedia.*[53]

Even Ravenscroft says the Maurice Lance dates back only to the third century, adding it had "apparently" been traced by "numerous historians" right through to the tenth century, without citing any sources for this assumption.[54]

It would take much research to examine each one of Ravenscroft's claims concerning the possessors of the Maurice Lance and its effect on them and on world history. Besides, we do not have the unique facility Ravenscroft had in tracing its owners where there is no written record: for example, its progression from the time it left the hands of Heinrich I and turned up many years later in the possession of his son Otto the Great. Ravenscroft says Hitler's henchman SS head Heinrich Himmler put the finest scholars in Germany to work on bridging the gap but they were unable to do so. However, Ravenscroft's mentor, Dr. Walter Stein, "by means of a unique method of historical research involving 'Mind Expansion' was able to discover Heinrich had sent the lance to the English King Athelstan." (Athelstan [895–940], was the grandson of Alfred the Great. Crowned King in 925, he was the first ruler of all England). Stein "found" that the lance was present at the Battle of Malmesbury in which the Danes were defeated on English soil. It was subsequently returned as a gift for Otto's wedding to Athelstan's sister Eadgita.[55]

Ravenscroft does not himself expand on Stein's unique method of mind control but it appears it may have caused Stein to mix up the lance with an equally famous sword! According to William of Malmesbury, one of the gifts that Hugh the Good, Duke of the Franks, sent to King Athelstan to persuade him to give his daughter's hand in marriage was "the sword of Constantine the Great, on which the name of the ancient owner could be read in letters of gold; on the pommel also could be seen an iron nail fixed above three plates of gold—one of the four the Jewish party prepared for the Crucifixion of our Lord's body."[56] A nail which is embedded in the blade of the Holy Lance in the Treasure House Museum in Vienna is also said to have been from the cross.

One more example concerning its ownership may suffice to show the problem involved in searching for the truth of Ravenscroft's historical claims. He talks of Constantine being guided by "Providence" to hold the lance at the battle of Milvian Bridge on the road to Rome (312 C.E.).[57] Constantine's victory in this battle is said to have led directly to his encouraging Christianity as the religion of Romans.

Apart from the fact that if Constantine was holding the Holy Lance it would make him the possessor of an object whose "survival" the record shows was not known until the sixth century (and if anyone knew of its existence beforehand it surely would have been Constantine), it is accepted that what inspired Constantine in this battle was not a lance, but visions of Christ and the cross.

There are various versions of the vision story: that Christ appeared to Constantine either in a dream or in broad daylight, or that angels spoke to Constantine and told him to create a battle standard in the form of a cross. Constantinian scholar John Holland Smith finds that the earliest and most credible version of what happened is that of Lactantius, a court attendant, which was written only a year or so after the events it describes.[58] Given the time it allegedly took before some of the gospels were compiled, it is very close indeed to the actual event.

Lactantius says that during the night before the battle of Milvian Bridge, Christ appeared to the emperor in a dream and declared *Hoc signo victor eris*: "By this sign you shall be the Victor." Christ directed that the sign, the letter *X* with a perpendicular line through it, be marked on the shields of Constantine's soldiers, this being His monogram.[59]

Constantine ascribed his victory to the quasi-magical powers of Christ's *X* symbol and from that time onward he let it be known that he regarded the faith of the Christians as that of free Romans.[60]

While we are considering the religious ramifications of this story we should look at the question of the lance as a holy relic. As relics go it would have to be one of the most precious, right up there with others that are worshipped, although their own authenticity is open to doubt: pieces from the true cross, the Shroud of Turin, and in some quarters the Holy Grail, the latter in its form as the cup or bowl that collected the blood of Christ and/ or was used in the Last Supper. But we have seen already how unlikely it is that the lance in the Hapsburg Museum is the original and that claims for other specimens are also doubtful. However, the phenomenon of the veneration of relics did not grow for some hundreds of years, until the Church was well and truly established, from around the fourth and fifth centuries[61] when, incidentally, it would have been more difficult for the authenticity of such items to be verified.

The collection, display, and worship of relics is given little justification in either the Old or New Testaments.[62] In other words, those implements associated with Christ at the time of his death would not have been then and for hundreds of years afterward considered holy and worthy of preservation, let alone reverence, which may explain why the lance and the so-called Holy Grail did not surface for a similar period.

Given all of the above, the chances that a genuine Holy Lance survived to this century to mentally transfix Hitler becomes even more improbable.

Notes

1. Trevor Ravenscroft, *The Spear of Destiny* (York Beach, Me.: Samuel Weiser Inc., 1982), p. xix.

2. *The Fontana Dictionary of Modern Thought* (London: Collins, 1977), p. 26.

3. Colin Wilson, *The Psychic Detectives* (London: Pan, 1984), p. 119.

4. Ibid.

5. See chapter 5.

6. Ravenscroft, *The Spear of Destiny*, p. 267.

7. Ibid., p. 263, n. 1.

8. See chapter 11.

9. Ibid., pp. 263–64.

10. Colin Wilson, *Rudolf Steiner: The Man and His Vision* (Wellingborough, Northamptonshire, U.K.: The Aquarian Press, 1985), p. 151.

11. Ibid.

12. See chapter 11.

13. Ravenscroft, *The Spear of Destiny*, pp. 288–89.

14. Wilson, *Rudolf Steiner*, p. 153, n. 7.

15. Ravenscroft, *The Spear of Destiny*, p. 47, n. 1.

16. Ibid., p. 48.

17. Ibid., p. 54.

18. Ibid.

19. Michael FitzGerald, *Storm Troopers of Satan* (London: Robert Hale, 1990), p. 33.

20. Francis King, *Satan and Swastika* (St. Albans, Herts, U.K.: Mayflower Books, 1976), p. 70.

21. FitzGerald, *Storm Troopers of Satan*, p. 33, n. 16.

22. Ravenscroft, *The Spear of Destiny*, p. 77, n. 1.

23. FitzGerald, *Storm Troopers of Satan*, p. 35.

24. Ravenscroft, *The Spear of Destiny*, p. 64.

25. FitzGerald, *Storm Troopers of Satan*, p. 31.

26. Ibid., p. 59.

27. Ravenscroft, *The Spear of Destiny*, pp. 64–65.

28. Ibid., pp. 67–68.

29. Percy E. Schramm, *Hitler: The Man and the Military Leader*, ed. and trans. Donald S. Detwiler (Chicago: Quadrangle, 1971), p. 205.

30. Albert Speer, *Inside the Third Reich* (New York: Macmillan, 1970), p. 575.

31. Ravenscroft, *The Spear of Destiny,* p. 67.

32. Ibid., p. 68.

33. Ibid., p. 60.

34. FitzGerald, *Storm Troopers of Satan,* p. 33.

35. Ibid., p. 37.

36. Ravenscroft, *The Spear of Destiny,* p. xx.

37. Ibid., p. xiii.

38. Ibid.

39. Ibid., p. xiv.

40. Ibid., p. xiii.

41. Ibid., p. xiv.

42. Ibid., p. xv.

43. F. L. Cross, ed., *The Oxford Dictionary of the Christian Church* (London, 1958), p. 783.

44. Ibid., n. 1

45. Ibid.

46. Editorial staff, The Catholic University of America, Washington, D.C., *New Catholic Encyclopedia,* vol. 7 (New York: McGraw-Hill, 1976), p. 76.

47. Cross, *The Oxford Dictionary of the Christian Church,* p. 783, n. 1.

48. *New Catholic Encyclopedia,* vol. 7, p. 76, n. 6.

49. Ibid., p. 76.

50. Ibid.

51. Cross, *The Oxford Dictionary of the Christian Church,* p. 783.

52. Ibid.

53. *New Catholic Encyclopedia,* vol. 7, p. 76.

54. Ravenscroft, *The Spear of Destiny,* p. 12.

55. Ibid., pp. 12–13.

56. Quoted by John Holland Smith, *Constantine the Great* (London: Hamish Hamilton, 1971), p. 325.

57. Ravenscroft, *The Spear of Destiny,* p. 14.

58. Smith, *Constantine the Great,* pp. 102–103.

59. Ibid., p. 103.

60. Ibid.

61. *New Catholic Encyclopedia,* vol. 12, p. 234.

62. Ibid.

7

Ravenscroft Meets Stein, and Goes to War

What do we know of Trevor Ravenscroft? His upbringing sounds typically British middle- to upper-class. Born in England in 1921, he attended the Repton Public School. He went from there to Sandhurst, Britain's Royal Military College (now Academy) in August 1939, and was commissioned into the Royal Scots Fusiliers within six months (30 December 1939). We are told he subsequently trained as a commando and joined Special Services.[1]

According to his published biographical notes, Ravenscroft was captured in a commando raid "which attempted to assassinate Field Marshal Rommel in North Africa" in 1941.[2] He spent the rest of the war either in prisoner-of-war camps in North Africa, Italy, and Germany or fleeing from them. In all, he escaped three times and each time was recaptured. However, according to another source, as a result of these attempts he was sent to a concentration camp and was at one point in a condemned block.[3]

When not escaping, Ravenscroft spent time in the camps attaining higher levels of consciousness through study and meditation. These transcendental experiences guided him to a study of the Holy Grail and to research the history of the Holy Lance and the "legend of world destiny which had grown around it."[4]

Any imaginative and sensitive young man finding himself involved in such an adventure followed by years in a POW camp could well have been moved to considerations of metaphysical thoughts on the meaning of existence, including the possibilities of the eternal struggle between Good and Evil.

None of the authorities* I researched mention Ravenscroft as one of the twenty-eight officers and men who took part in the Rommel raid on 13–14 November 1941. All except two of the party who landed on the Libyan coast were captured. Rommel himself, the sources agree, was, in any case, nowhere near the scene.

One who did take part in the raid, the former Commando Sergeant Jack Terry, who now lives in Bulwell, Nottingham, England, insisted Ravenscroft was not a member of the party.†

In any case Ravenscroft's service record‡ shows he was "missing at sea" on 24 October 1941, well before the raid. He was subsequently taken a prisoner of war on an unspecified date.

Ravenscroft's brother, Bill, explained this anomalous episode by saying Ravenscroft had been captured during a *reconnaissance* mission to the Rommel headquarters in North Africa. As both an ex-journalist and ex-army officer Bill Ravenscroft would be well aware of the distinct difference between a reconnaissance, a search in the field for useful military intelligence, and a raid, a sudden attack on the enemy by a small force.

Despite the explicit words in the biographical note on the covers of both the paperback and hardcover editions of his book, Ravenscroft himself in the text is ambiguous about his involvement in the raid: "I was telling him (Stein) one day about the attempted assassination of General Rommel in North Africa and mentioned that I had served in the Commandos with Lt-Colonel Geoffrey Keyes, V.C., who led the raid."[5]

Ravenscroft may have claimed that the biographical notes on

---

*Barrie Pitt, *The Crucible of War* (London: Jonathan Cape, 1980); Wolf Helmann, *Rommel's War in Africa* (London: Granada, 1981); and Ward Rutherford, *The Biography of Field Marshal Erwin Rommel* (London: Hamlyn, 1981).

†Letter to author from Sgt. Terry dated 22 September 1993.

‡Issued by the United Kingdom Ministry of Defence, 8 August 1991.

the cover of the American paperback edition of his book were inaccurate. If so, he had ample opportunity to correct it in subsequent editions and appears not to have done so. Authors are generally asked to check such material for accuracy before publication. However, as noted, the claim of his taking part in the raid is also made in the biographical notes on the jacket of the American hardcover edition of his book using exactly the same words (that he was "captured in a raid which attempted to assassinate Field Marshal Rommel in North Africa in 1941, escaping three times, etc."). Once again it appears Ravenscroft did not bother to ask for a correction from G. P. Putnam & Sons of New York, the hardcover publishers before publication, or afterwards from Samuel Weiser. In other words, it appears that he was happy with the impression of his role as a participant in the Rommel raid.

In a taped interview with Ravenscroft in Australia,* he talked briefly of his time in the Commandos in which "I had been engaged in unique raids and training for killing people."

Ravenscroft went on to wax philosophical about his years as a POW, which forced him into a self-knowledge. "From being a very objective exoteric person I suddenly began to search within the anatomy of inner space for other realities which I became incredibly interested in," he recalled.

He had been a clairvoyant as a child, seeing spiritual beings which were not connected with the earth. "It was like living in a fairyland," he said, adding, "it was a great surprise to me that others didn't see these things." This experience—Rudolf Steiner

---

*A member of the Theosophical Society bookshop staff in Sydney, Australia, offered the tape to the author in 1993 as an aid to his research into this book. The tape contains few identifying details—the interviewer is not named, for example. The staff member said he had obtained a copy from a customer who was also uncertain of its origin. But from further inquiries it appears the interview was done during a seminar Ravenscroft held in Melbourne, Australia, in 1986. The author gave a copy to Ravenscroft's brother, Bill, who identified the voice as that of Trevor Ravenscroft.

had similar experiences as a child—presented him with an open door to the spiritual revelations he was seeking while a POW, he added.

After the war Ravenscroft seems to have had a mixed and restless career. He studied medicine at St. Thomas Hospital, London, during which time he met Walter Stein. Their meeting came about a few years after the war. Ravenscroft had come to believe that a book Stein had written on the historical background of the Holy Grail was done with the aid of some form of transcendent faculty similar to that which had inspired Wolfram von Eschenbach to write his famous twelfth-century Grail romance *Parsifal*.[6] Much of the historical material used in the book had come "through some quite new technique of historical research involving the use of occult faculties and the practice of mind expansion."[7]

(The occult historian Francis King scornfully dismisses Stein and in so doing, Ravenscroft, by saying that the latter's book *The Spear of Destiny* seems to have been very largely based upon the clairvoyant investigations of Stein "whose main claim to fame rests upon his authorship of an eccentric treatise entitled *World History in the Light of the Holy Grail*."[8])

Determined to verify his deduction, Ravenscroft paid Stein an unannounced visit at his Kensington, London, home. Ravenscroft quickly got to the point, saying that Eschenbach was indicating past events of history were recoverable by means of higher faculties. Eschenbach himself had demonstrated these faculties and he believed Stein, too, had discovered them.[9]

Ravenscroft quoted to Stein this extract from Eschenbach's work: "If anyone requests me to do so (continue the story) let him not consider it as a book. I don't know a single letter of the alphabet." Ravenscroft says that the reason Eschenbach was stressing that he did not know a letter of the alphabet was to make it clear that he had not gathered the material for the book from his contemporaries, traditional folklore, or any existing written work. Rather, he was saying his so-called Grail romance was an "Initiation Document" of the highest order.[10]

Ravenscroft told Stein that he believed "that the legend associated with the (Holy Lance) had been inspired by 'its singular effect as a catalyst of revelation into those very secrets of *Time*,' " out of which Stein had written his book.[11] Stein's response to all this was to ask Ravenscroft to stay to lunch. It was the beginning of a friendship that was to last until Stein's death.

Ravenscroft's career changes continued: He became a journalist. At one stage he worked as an adviser to the Shah of Iran, although it is not known in what capacity.

In the introduction to his interview in Australia Ravenscroft is described as "the world's leading metaphysical historian, a giant of a man in his field, the twentieth century's greatest authority of the search for the Grail." As with the raid story, Ravenscroft neither confirms nor denies these plaudits.

Ravenscroft told the Australian interviewer he was very much influenced by Dr. Stein's incredible knowledge of the Initiation Sciences. He believed he had taken further than Dr. Stein "the techniques of raising the consciousness and perceiving not only the physical world with one's physical senses but the spiritual world as well." In other words, Ravenscroft had improved not only on Stein's theories, but also on those of Steiner.

In March 1979, Ravenscroft won a United Kingdom High Court lawsuit against another author in an action involving plagiarism. Ravenscroft, then fifty-eight, alleged that James Herbert had infringed on the copyright of *The Spear of Destiny*.

In the Chancery Division, Mr. Justice Brightman held that Herbert had done this in his novel *The Spear* "to a substantial extent." In his findings published in the *British Law Court Report* on 8 May 1980, the judge said that Herbert, thirty-six, had done so "to give his novel a backbone of truth with the least possible labor to himself."

Justice Brightman, reviewing *The Spear,* said the book was a thriller, weaving an improbable story of neo-Hitler terrorism in England around the spear post-World War II. After outlining the plot he said, "One must not underestimate the commercial attraction of the rubbish I have attempted to describe. The book

is written with much inventiveness and a racy flow of language."
On the other hand, the judge said Ravenscroft's book combined
historical fact with a great deal of mysticism and purported to
tell the history of the lance from the earliest times down to the
end of World War II. "The reason that battle has been joined
is that Mr. Herbert is alleged to have made extensive use of the
plaintiff's nonfiction work in order to paint a backcloth of apparent
truth against which his own fiction story can be narrated."

The judge said the Ravenscroft book was "discursive and
disjointed and demands of the reader considerable effort and
concentration. It is packed with an immense amount of historical
data which no one suggests are in any way inaccurate."

For obvious reasons neither side in the case argued the accuracy
or otherwise of the "data" to be found in Ravenscroft's book.

Also apparently uncontested in this case was the story of
Ravenscroft's war record. Brightman notes that Ravenscroft joined
the commandos and was "taken prisoner after a raid on Rommel's
Headquarters in North Africa." He gives the number of
Ravenscroft's escape attempts as two and not three as in other
reports. Ravenscroft naturally gave evidence, but not evidence that
contradicted the story of his taking part in this much-vaunted raid
on Rommel.

Going over the evidence presented to him, the judge mentioned
the story of how Stein had met Hitler, had gone on to serve as
an officer in the Austrian army in World War I, opposed the
rise to power of the Nazis, "and for this purpose" infiltrated a
Nazi secret society called the *Thule Gesselschaft*. In 1933 he had
fled from Germany to England where he had built up a medical
practice in London.

Of Ravenscroft's meeting with Stein, the judge said:

During his time as a prisoner of war the plaintiff (Ravenscroft)
had become interested in what has been described to me as
supernatural levels of consciousness, which means learning about
past facts through meditation. This interest led him to a study
of medieval European history and, in particular, of the legends
surrounding the Holy Grail. In the course of his reading he

came across a book written by Dr. Stein . . . a study of the historical background of the Grail romances. The plaintiff was much impressed by this book. He thought Dr. Stein had achieved these supernatural levels of consciousness which so much interested him. He sought the acquaintance of Dr. Stein and a close friendship developed between them. Stein indeed believed that he had the power to recapture lost moments of history by meditation, and he found a ready listener in the plaintiff. Their friendship began in the year 1948. Their discussion ranged over a wide field, including medieval and modern European history, contemporary politics, and medicine. Although each was working, the plaintiff as a journalist and Dr. Stein as a doctor. Their homes were close together in Kensington and they would meet in the evenings. . . .

Dr. Stein unfolded to the plaintiff the story of the spear, as he claimed to have traced it, partly by orthodox historical study and partly by meditation, beginning in pre-Christian times and continuing to the present day.

The plaintiff did not make anything approaching a full record of what was told him by Dr. Stein. He did not, at that time, have any notion of himself writing a book about the Hofburg Spear. He did, however, keep a diary from time to time and he also made separate notes for future reference. However, one evening in 1957, Dr. Stein telephoned the plaintiff and asked him to call. There is some evidence, though it is inconclusive, that Dr. Stein had a few days previously, made up his mind to compose his own book about the spear. However that may be, on that evening, Dr. Stein told the plaintiff that it was he who would have to write the story of the Hofburg Spear. They had a long session together, the plaintiff returning home in the early hours of the morning. It was the last time they met. Dr. Stein was taken ill next day and shortly afterwards died in hospital. The plaintiff believes that Dr. Stein had a premonition of his early death.

A disparity in the story of how Ravenscroft's *Spear* came to be written appears to have been revealed. Ravenscroft in his book does not specifically say that Stein told him at any stage it would be up to him to do the writing, only that the task fell to him and Stein would almost certainly have written it but for his untimely death.[12] He does not say the mantle was handed to him by Stein, which may be a reason why Ravenscroft, as the author of the story, was not apparently universally accepted among Stein's friends as we shall see.

The judge said that it was not until 1969 that Ravenscroft started to write the book. He spent two years on the task devoting all his time to it and making use of Dr. Stein's earlier book, his own records, his recollections of what Stein had told him twelve or more years earlier, and his own notes on medieval history. He traveled extensively and studied in the British Museum library and elsewhere.

The judge records that Ravenscroft was incensed when the Corgi paperback edition of his book was published in 1974 because the cover was a picture of a diminutive Hitler wearing a sort of red Roman toga and holding the spear and a swastika shield, depicted against a lurid background of Hitler's face in electric blue. This was not the sort of impression Ravenscroft desired his book to give to the potential reader and had been done without his approval while he was in America.

Judge Brightman notes that the defendant Herbert agreed he had no independent knowledge of medieval history and did no research of his own. One can only speculate as to what Herbert's attitude and approach might have been had he done some research and uncovered facts such as those outlined on these pages. As the judge said, the main thrust of the defense counsel's argument was that Ravenscroft intended his book to be read as a factual account of historical events, that the defendant accepted it as fact and did no more than repeat certain of those facts. The plaintiff, he went on, cannot claim a monopoly in historical facts.

Toward the end of his judgment, Mr. Justice Brightman made this point:

> The purpose of a novel is usually to interest the reader and to contribute to his enjoyment and leisure. A historical work may well have that purpose, but the author of a serious and original historical work may properly be assumed by his readers

to have another purpose as well, namely to add to the knowledge possessed by the reader and perhaps in the process to increase the sum total of human experience and understanding.

The judge granted Ravenscroft, then of Castle Road, Dartmouth, a declaration against Herbert and his publishers, New English Library, that they had substantially infringed on his copyright.

Some six months before the court case, Ravenscroft was involved in another drama. It began in 1976 when he moved with his ailing wife, Shirley, then fifty-two, from London to Dartmouth in Devon in the south of England. Over the next two years the healthier airs and a better diet produced an almost miraculous recovery in Mrs. Ravenscroft, who had been a virtual invalid, crippled with arthritis and unable to work.

To celebrate her recovery and her love of the sea, Shirley, then a grandmother, set out on 5 October 1978 in a 26-foot yacht on a solo voyage across the Atlantic, destination New York. Her trip had been financed by Trevor at a cost of 14,000 pounds sterling ($29,780 U.S.). However, days later, she was caught in a force 10 gale and knocked unconscious as huge waves swamped the yacht and smashed her radio equipment. When she came to she was bleeding from a head wound and with an injured arm and leg was forced to pump almost nonstop for two days to keep the yacht afloat.

When the storm abated Shirley hoisted sails and made it to Lisbon where she received medical treatment and called Trevor. After speaking to her he told the *Daily Telegraph*: "It's incredible she is alive—by right she should have drowned. Any other woman her age would have been a goner. But Shirley showed amazing determination. She told me she had originally thought she had broken her arm and leg in the fall. Luckily they were only badly bruised. There's no telling how long she was unconscious—but it must have been for a considerable time."[13]

Ravenscroft wrote a second book, *The Cup of Destiny,* about the Holy Grail, in which he related his views of its relevance throughout history and its significance today, claiming it could be used to develop spiritual facilities and obtain a higher level of consciousness.

Ravenscroft died in the early morning of 3 January 1989, in Roncroft Hospice, Torquay, England, of cancer.

In October 1994 I spoke to Ravenscroft's widow, Shirley, who now uses the surname Griffin. Before we got down to talking about her late husband, I asked about her ordeal in the yacht. She laughingly dismissed the incident as being nothing special. She had overcome her surprise and was giving every indication of being friendly and forthright.

I tentatively mentioned the commando raid and Ms. Griffin was soon in full flight, as though she had told the story a thousand times before. What she related was very little different from the story on the jacket of *The Spear*: how as a very young man Trevor, who had lied about his age to join the army, had taken part in the commando raid whose object was to assassinate Rommel and had himself been captured. He had been taken to Italy and suffered a near fatal bout of dysentery. He had escaped three times but had been captured each time. It was obvious Ms. Griffin believed every word of the story.

I asked: "Had the details of his capture and subsequent imprisonment been noted in his war record given you in 1991?"

"I got some details, but nobody will say very much," she responded, adding, "You have to understand he was one of the very first commandos to go into action. It was early in the war, a hectic time. I don't suppose at that time there were many records kept."

I resisted the urge to tell her what I had learned about the raid from other sources. The Ravenscrofts had met and married in 1953 and had four children. She was obviously still fond of husband Trevor and had believed his war story for a very long time. I felt it was neither the time nor the place for me to say anything that may disillusion her. I had more questions to ask and did not know if her mood was subject to sudden change or even in her present mood how long she would be willing to continue talking about their relationship and the book. Perhaps she had been badly treated in previous interviews!

Given that there had been no reply to my letters, I had no

idea when I dialed her number how this unexpected call was going to work out. But she continued to talk willingly: how her husband's interest in philosophy and Eastern religions was aroused as a result of coming under the guiding influence of a fellow POW who was a professor of philosophy in civilian life. He had also come across a book by Steiner.

Shortly after the war Trevor was experiencing "all kinds of problems and was undergoing medical treatment. . . . At the time they could not tell what his problems were, but these days it would be called some kind of post-traumatic shock as a result of his experiences as a prisoner of war."

Stein, she revealed, had treated her husband medically at this time. "He was a bit of an alchemist," she confided. Stein, she went on, meant a great deal to Trevor "probably as much as anyone else in the world."

And what did she think of Dr. Stein?

"I never met Dr. Stein. . . . I heard a great deal about him from Trevor."

At the time of their marriage, Ravenscroft was seeing Stein on an almost daily basis and continued to do so for the next three years. Yet he had never introduced his wife to the man who meant so much to him! Ms. Griffin did not seem to find this unusual.

Did her husband at any stage express doubts about what Stein had told him, in particular his relationship with Hitler?

"Never, at any stage."

Shirley said the book had been a bestseller in many countries and had enabled them to travel widely, exploring and studying other places and philosophies.

Ms. Griffin said she was by profession an educator. She was a follower of Steiner's teachings. She had contemplated writing a biography of her husband but was having the same trouble I appeared to be having in gathering information.

What had this interview given me? If nothing else it had made it obvious that the source of Ravenscroft's role in "the Rommel assassination attempt" was not some book-blurb writer or publicist, but Ravenscroft himself. Furthermore, it showed his state of mind when he was with Stein. Whatever his condition, it could hardly be said to be normal and must certainly have been impressionable rather than objective. Shirley Griffin made some final comments that appear to indicate Stein may not necessarily have expected Ravenscroft to write of his (Stein's) experiences. She said friends of Stein had been critical of some aspects of *The Spear* and did not think a journalist, which Ravenscroft then was, was a suitable person to undertake the task. However, she did not elaborate.

Ravenscroft's brother, Bill, a retired journalist, is now a resident of Cape Coral, Florida.

In January 1995, the ex-King's Own Borderers officer willingly and with as much objectivity as he could muster gave me details of his younger brother for whom he still obviously feels deep affection. What he had to say throws open to doubt much of the accepted story of how the *Spear* came to be written and whether Ravenscroft believed some of his most contentious claims.

I should explain that Bill Ravenscroft is legally blind so responded to my queries on audio tape.

Major Ravenscroft's story of how Trevor came to write the *Spear* differs markedly from that found in the book. It appears Trevor met Dr. Stein not by calling upon him unannounced as he claimed (see earlier in this chapter) but through Stein's wife, Yopi. The meeting with Yopi came about when Trevor was teaching at the Rudolf Steiner school in East Grinstead shortly after the war. "Yopi helped to further Trevor's education in anthroposophy, that's how Trevor met her," said Bill. (*Anthroposophy*—literally "wisdom about man"—was a term adopted by Steiner to denote his teachings.)

He went on: "That's how he learned of Dr. Stein's library and that's how he got in there and found the works he needed to complete *The Spear*. I believe it was some time at the end of the fifties that Trevor got permission from Yopi to delve into Dr. Stein's library." Bill Ravenscroft said he had personally met Yopi, "a very interesting person" who had spent some time in Japan. However, like Trevor's wife, he never met the enigmatic

Dr. Stein. Trevor had told him that Stein was a friend of Winston Churchill.

Apart from the variation in the story of the Ravenscroft-Stein encounter, one of the most intriguing points to emerge from this revelation is the fact that Trevor makes no mention of Yopi in *The Spear*. Why? Was Bill's memory of events incorrect? Was it because the symbiotic relationship that supposedly developed between Trevor and the man he claims was his mentor never happened? Time may well have hidden the answers.

Bill Ravenscroft recalls that his brother arrived in New York in the late sixties with the manuscript of *The Spear*. Bill was manager of the *London Daily Express* New York bureau syndication service. Trevor had been working for the same newspaper in London. "We found him a literary agent in New York and Putnam's eventually published it and then it was picked up in England," said Bill, adding wryly: "He was riding high financially for quite a while."

Why did he not choose to have it published originally in Britain? Had the manuscript been rejected by British publishers? Had he been unsuccessful in finding a British agent? Or had he simply decided to start at the top in the far bigger American market?

It is obvious that he did well with *The Spear,* and that its publication was a turning point in Trevor's life. From being a journalist with an unfocused outlook, he suddenly found himself in demand in the alternative lifestyle of the New Age world. He "held court" in Morocco with "American students" and others interested in metaphysics, and was in residence at Findhorn, Scotland, many times throughout the seventies and eighties, traveling to the United States and other countries on lecture tours. He also spent time in Hollywood attempting to sell the film rights to *The Spear*. He never succeeded despite a couple of near hits, says Bill.

His brother paints a picture of a below-average student blossoming in maturity into "undoubtedly a tremendous scholar of esoteric studies." Having made that claim, Bill comes up with the startling observation: "I was never really sure whether Trevor took the occult side of Hitler with a pinch of salt. I think that in some parts of *The Spear* there is a little bit of Trevor Ravenscroft in there when it gets around to talking about black magic." In other words, Trevor made it up!

This raises the question: How can Bill argue a case for his brother's scholarly credentials—"you could not find anybody who was more scholarly in his particular field"—and claim one of his major works of fact was, in its essential parts, a figment of that scholar's imagination? As we have seen, Mr. Justice Brightman observed that *The Spear* was packed with an immense amount of historical data that no one suggested were in any way inaccurate. It is also apt to recall the judge further observed that a historical work is assumed to be for the purpose of adding to the knowledge of its reader and perhaps increasing the sum total of human experience and understanding.

Bill's memory may be inaccurate in parts. For example, he claims his brother came to New York in the late sixties with the manuscript, while the court in England heard that Trevor did not start to write the book until 1969. But, as he says, I was asking him to look back over fifty years of events. However, the tone and approach of Major Ravenscroft is to set the record straight to the best of his abilities. He comes across as forthright and honest while expressing sympathy for the physical and mental suffering his brother endured in his formative years as a POW which, says Bill, affected him for the rest of his life.

In summary, Bill reveals discrepancies in the story of a man and his work. Through *The Spear* and his teachings there are many who today believe Trevor Ravenscroft was a man of apocalyptic revelation who provides unique insight into the monster of the twentieth century and esoteric wisdom. That the Rommel story, the fateful meeting between the author and Stein, and the broad hint that Ravenscroft's claim of Hitler's involvement in "monstrous sadistic" magic rituals were quite possibly a product of Trevor Ravenscroft's imagination shakes those credentials.

Notes

1. Compiled from publisher's notes on both U.S. hardcover and paperback edition covers of Trevor Ravenscroft's *The Spear of Destiny* and also records from the Royal Military Academy Central Library, Camberley, Surrey.

2. Ibid., cover notes.

3. Quoted by interviewer in interview with Trevor Ravenscroft, Australia, 1986.

4. Ibid., Ravenscroft to interviewer.

5. Trevor Ravenscroft, *The Spear of Destiny* (York Beach, Me.: Samuel Weiser Inc., 1982), p. xx.

6. See chapter 6.

7. Ravenscroft, *The Spear of Destiny,* p. xv.

8. Francis King, *Satan and Swastika* (St. Albans, Herts, U.K.: Mayflower Books, 1976), p. 13.

9. Ravenscroft, *The Spear of Destiny,* pp. xv–xvii.

10. Ibid., p. xvii.

11. Ibid., p. xix.

12. *Daily Telegraph,* 30 October 1978.

13. Trevor Ravenscroft, interview, Australia, 1986.

8

Hitler and the Opera

In his youth Hitler had been a chorister at Lambach in Upper Austria and many years later could still sing the Mozart masses from memory.[1] Both Alan Bullock and Joachim Fest note a seldom mentioned aspect of Hitler's musical tastes: He enjoyed attending the light operas of the Hungarian composer Franz Lehar. Among Lehar's works are *The Merry Widow, Frederico,* and *The Land of Smiles.* Hitler could sit through endless performances of *Die Lustige Fledermaus,* says Fest.[2] As a result of his interest, throughout his adult life he could be heard humming airs from Lehar.

However, the music that most inspired him was that of the nineteenth-century composer Richard Wagner. Hitler kept in his Munich apartment the silver-knobbed black walking cane with which Nietzsche strolled the banks of Lake Geneva with Wagner,[3] no doubt arguing their ultimately diverging views on the super race that both fervently believed, as Hitler did, would one day rule the world. The cane served as a satisfying symbol of Hitler's identification with two of his heroes.

The "make-believe world of opera" enabled Hitler to hang on to his early adolescence, an inner world of carefree existence and narcissistic yielding to personal interest.[4]

Some conclusions made in 1993 by Professor Wayne Koestanbaum may throw a new light on this passion, although this is not the place to explore them in detail. Briefly, the professor argues that opera is an extension of gayness and an inextricable part of gay behavior. While Koestanbaum acknowledges that heterosexuals derive great enjoyment from opera, he believes that even that interest shows signs of latent homosexuality. Hitler, whose sexuality is so much in question, went without eating to save the money for opera tickets, and could remember in detail the performances of all the operas he had seen.[5] Furthermore, the young Hitler in Vienna, knowing little about many things and nothing about musical composition, took up an idea Wagner had dropped and began writing an opera "full of bloody and incestuous nonsense."[6] Like so much that Hitler poured his restless energy into in those days, it came to nothing.

As opera lovers know, the Holy Lance plays a significant role in Wagner's *Parsifal,* which was Hitler's favorite. Yet we are told Hitler knew nothing of the lance or its legend until the guide mentioned it that rainy day in the museum.[7]

From Ravenscroft we are to believe Hitler had not seen the opera: he had "to wait several months until it was presented at the Vienna Opera House."[8] Before doing so Hitler researched the story of *Parsifal,* Wagner's last great work to which he dedicated the final years of his life from 1877 to 1882.[9] He took as the theme the struggle between the Knights of the Holy Grail and their adversary the evil magician Klingsor over possession of the Holy Grail and Holy Lance. The lance falls into the hands of Sir Parsifal who causes Klingsor and his castle to vanish by making the sign of the cross with it. As its possessor Parsifal is anointed King of the Holy Grail.[10] Whenever it was that he did see the opera and read *Parsifal,* Hitler should have realized as a result an obvious point: there is a vast and significant difference between the two in both spirit and plot.

> Wagner's *Parsifal,* splendid as it may be musically, is, as a literary work, a pretentiously moralizing opera libretto, wholly alien in spirit to the work it professes to dramatize.[11]

Ravenscroft indicates that Hitler made no such distinction.[12] He claims that within the verses of the Middle Ages romantic work Hitler believed he had discovered a specific "Western path to the attainment of transcendent consciousness and new levels of Time (sic) experience."[13] This would have been about the time Hitler was futilely turning the discarded Wagner opera into something "full of bloody and incestuous nonsense."

Even before he went to Vienna, young Hitler in the provincial city of Linz had succumbed to Wagner and there were periods when he went to the opera night after night.[14] Bullock says that during this time Hitler was left spellbound by the music of his great hero, Wagner.[15] It is pretty obvious, then, that the major flaw in Ravenscroft's assertions regarding Hitler and *Parsifal* is his claim that Hitler lacked knowledge of Wagner's best-known opera at the time he first confronted the Holy Lance.

Whether Hitler *understood* the material is another question. Ravenscroft says Hitler was upset at the Christian message in Wagner's work.[16] If so, he missed an essential element to an understanding of it: The church has never recognized the Holy Grail and, as we have seen, does not put much stock in the various claimants for the lance,[17] both symbols which are so much a part of the story of Parsifal.*

> Grave objections confront those who would have the Grail Holy and Christian . . . and no wise pagan; the Grail of the romances such as *Parsifal* is found in a castle, not in a church, a king not a priest is its keeper and a female carries it, contrary to all church usage.[18]

Bullock shows that even more important than legend or plot to Hitler was Wagner's personality and the romantic conception of the artist as a genius, which Wagner himself had largely created.[19]

There are two obvious points to be made from this: (1) it was not the legend or whether Wagner's *Parsifal* was based on that legend—even whether Klingsor was Hitler's so-called rein-

---

*Even though the spearhead of one of the claimants is kept in St. Peter's, Rome, the Catholic church emphasizes that its authenticity has always been doubted.

carnation of Landulf—that really moved Hitler; it was the music and its staging; and (2) Hitler admired Wagner for his unreality and his theatricality, not to mention his anti-Semitism!

Furthermore, an objective researcher must find it difficult to imagine Hitler's unruly mental processes permitting him to formulate a philosophy based on the complex verses of Eschenbach.

Once while in a euphoric mood, Hitler asked that a record of *Parsifal* be played: Hitler made the comment that he had built his own religion from it.[20] He had built a "religion." It required heroic worship: it was a theatrical religion, for display purposes, not one hidden in the occult or black magic. In Hitler's religion the sound and fury seduced the words. The heroic scenes inspired by Wagner were played out at Nazi rallies which slipped the boundaries of language to provide a new level of mass communication: its meaning was plotless; its imagery emerged as inflamed, base emotions. It is obvious that this is what Hitler responded to and why he appreciated Wagner: he never understood *Parsifal* or the symbolism of the role the Holy Lance played in the story. Ravenscroft's understanding is also arguable, as we shall see.

Notes

1. David Irving, *The War Path* (London: Michael Joseph, 1978), p. 227.

2. Joachim C. Fest, *Hitler* (Hammondsworth, Middlesex, U.K.: Pelican Books, 1977), p. 771.

3. Irving, *The War Path,* p. 55.

4. Edleff Schwaab, *Hitler's Mind: A Plunge into Madness* (New York: Praeger, 1992), p. 106.

5. Wayne Koestanbaum, *The Queen's Throat: Homosexuality and the Mystery of Desire,* cited by Alex Mitchell in his London notebook, *Sun-Herald,* 28 March 1983.

6. Fest, *Hitler,* p. 49.

7. See chapter 3.

8. Trevor Ravenscroft, *The Spear of Destiny* (York Beach, Me.: Samuel Weiser Inc., 1982), p. 33.

9. *Phaidon Book of the Opera* (Oxford: Oxford Publishing Company, 1979), pp. 284–85.

10. Ibid.

11. Helen Mustard and Charles Passage, Introduction to Wolfram von Eschenbach, *Parzival* (New York: Vintage Books, 1961), p. xiv.

12. Ravenscroft, *The Spear of Destiny*, p. 33.

13. Ibid.

14. Fest, *Hitler*, p. 37.

15. Alan Bullock, *Hitler and Stalin: Parallel Lives* (London: HarperCollins, 1991), p. 7.

16. Ravenscroft, *The Spear of Destiny*, p. 34.

17. See chapter 5.

18. Mustard and Passage, Introduction to Von Eschenbach, *Parzival*, p. xii.

19. Bullock, *Hitler and Stalin*, p. 80.

20. Hans Frank, *Im Angesicht des Galgens*, quoted in Fest, *Hitler*, p. 741.

9

Hitler and *Parsifal*

As we have seen in chapter 7, at their initial meeting Ravenscroft quoted to Stein some words from Wolfram von Eschenbach's twelfth-century Grail romance *Parsifal.* "If anyone requests me to do so (continue the story) let him not consider it as a book. I don't know a single letter of the alphabet."[1]

According to Ravenscroft, the reason Eschenbach was stressing that he did not know a letter of the alphabet was to make it quite clear that he had not gathered the material for the book from his contemporaries, traditional folklore, or any existing written work. Rather he was saying his so-called Grail romance was an "Initiation Document" of the highest order.[2] Although Ravenscroft does not expand on this phrase, he appears to be indicating that *Parsifal* offered an introduction into the occultic world for those who came to understand its symbolic as opposed to its literal meaning.

What Ravenscroft fails to mention and what Stein, if he is the source for this claim, should have mentioned in this initial encounter was that the passage has long presented others who have studied Eschenbach's work with what Helen Mustard and Charles Passage describe as "a crucial, unsolved, and probably unsolvable question."[3] The latter sentence of the quote would seem to mean, in its original early German, not a divine source for the whole work (as Ravenscroft asserts), but simply and plainly

"I don't know how to read or write"![4] One school of critics denies emphatically that an illiterate could have composed *Parsifal*: they explain the words as meaning that Eschenbach knew no Latin or that he was scoffing at the verse of a contemporary.

On the other hand, the many references to the source work involve expressions such as "as I heard it told."[5]

In their argument that Eschenbach was in fact illiterate, Mustard and Passage say folklore researchers in all parts of the world agree that "prodigious amounts of material are committed to memory by singers and reciters and in the face of such evidence there is the possibility that Eschenbach composed orally—just as *Parsifal* is obviously intended to be recited."[6] They insisted the poem reads like an oral work.

> The scenes, the pauses, the transitions, and above all the asides convey the impression of oral delivery caught, as it were, by an agile taker of shorthand. Gradually we form a concept of Wolfram, not as a poet or author, but as a public reciter and entertainer who delivered his recitations for sheer love of the story and for the glorification of the knightly class.[7]

Theirs is a far more prosaic—not to mention more scholarly— argument than Ravenscroft's and, for the not so occult-minded, more plausible. It is also an explanation with which Hitler, the master orator of the twentieth century, would have had some sympathy if we accept him as a dyslexic[8] who made up for it by memorizing prodigious amounts of diverse material that he could recite effortlessly. As we have seen, he could quote Schopenhauer by the page and Nietzsche, the other German philosopher of willpower, was also often on his lips.[9]

Wolfram von Eschenbach's version of *Parsifal* is not only the most famous but appears to be generally accepted as the most reliable of the Grail romances. Eschenbach, it seems, was a knight of Bavarian origins as well as a meistersinger, a traveling entertainer. He explains that his story was based on information from a Kyot de Provence who received it in turn from one Flegetanis.

Eschenbach writes:

Kyot, the well-known master, found in Toledo, discarded, set down in heathen writing, the first source of this adventure. He first had to learn the abc's but without the art of black magic. . . .

A heathen, Flegetanis, had achieved high renown for his learning. This scholar of nature was descended from Solomon and born of a family which had long been Israelites until baptism became our shield against the fire of Hell. He wrote the adventure of the Grail. . . .

The heathen Flegetanis could tell us how all the stars set and rise again . . . to the circling course of the stars man's affairs and destiny are linked. Flegetanis the heathen saw with his own eyes in the constellations things he was shy to talk about, hidden mysteries. He said there was a thing called the Grail, whose name he had read clearly in the constellations. A host of angels left it on the earth.

Since then baptized men have the task of guarding it, and with such chaste discipline that those who are called to the service of the Grail are always noble men.[10]

Mustard and Passage argue that the illiterate Eschenbach memorized the Parsifal verses, and point out that Eschenbach does not use the words "I read" or any other words that could signify he had, in fact, read the material. But with Kyot he expressly and pointedly says that *he* read the original story. Carrying this theory to its logical end Kyot or an intermediary would have had to read aloud to Wolfram from a manuscript, publicly or privately, or would have had to narrate in prose summary the total contents of the sixteen books. Eschenbach would have had to retain all that information while he worked out his own version over a period of years, and would finally have had to dictate the total work in sections presumably to one or more scribes.[11]

One point that stands out in the details of how Eschenbach came to hear of the Grail is that the story appears to be of Jewish origin: "This scholar . . . was descended from Solomon and born of a family which had long been Israelites. . . . He wrote the adventure of the Grail. . . ." It is a point Ravenscroft also implies regarding the Holy Lance: It may have been an ancient Jewish talisman of power.[12]

The authors of *Holy Blood, Holy Grail*—Michael Baigent, Richard Leigh, and Henry Lincoln—contend that the Israelite family can be traced back to a certain Laziliez, a name which may have derived from Lazarus.[13] They go on to say that Lazarus was the real identity of the "John" on whose testimony the fourth gospel was compiled.[14] John, as we have seen, is the only gospel that mentions the Holy Lance.

In their startling bestseller which rocked Christendom when it appeared in 1982, these authors hypothesize that Jesus had been married to Mary Magdalene and that they had a number of children which Mary took with her to France.[15] Thiering, in her later work, says specifically that Jesus and Mary Magdalene married and had children.[16]

Baigent et al. assert that the descendants who survive in Europe to this day—Jesus' bloodline—are symbolized by the Holy Grail.[17] A mysterious organization behind the bloodline has objectives today which would include a theocratic United States of Europe.[18] What they are talking about is a united Europe ruled by a dynasty descended from Jesus. This dynasty would not only occupy a throne of political and secular power, but, quite conceivably, the throne of St. Peter as well.[19]

Should the authors prove to be correct—and they must now be feeling some confidence that Europe is marching toward the unity allegedly sought by the descendants and the secret organization behind them—the Continent would be under the sway of part-descendants of the race Hitler sought to eliminate from that very landmass! Not only that, the source of their supposed occult powers would be the secrets that Ravenscroft tells us Hitler sought to harness. This can be added to the irony already noted: the strong evidence that the legend of *Parsifal,* on which Hitler claimed he had built his religion, may have been of Jewish origin. Through his "worship" of *Parsifal,* Hitler could be regarded by history as a victim of one of its greatest ironies.

Notes

1. Quoted by Trevor Ravenscroft, *The Spear of Destiny* (York Beach, Me.: Samuel Weiser Inc., 1982), p. xvii.

2. Ibid.

3. Helen Mustard and Charles Passage, Introduction, Wolfram von Eschenbach, *Parzival* (New York: Vintage Books, 1961), p. xix.

4. Ibid.

5. Ibid.

6. Ibid.

7. Ibid., p. xxi.

8. See chapters 6 and 7.

9. Norman Cameron and R. H. Stevens, *Hitler's Table Talk 1941–44* (London: Weidenfeld and Nicholson, 1953). See introduction, p. xxix.

10. Quoted by Michael Baigent, Richard Leigh, and Henry Lincoln, *The Holy Blood and the Holy Grail* (London: Jonathan Cape, 1982), pp. 306–307.

11. Mustard and Passage, Introduction to Von Eschenbach, *Parzival,* p. xx.

12. Ravenscroft, *The Spear of Destiny,* p. x.

13. Baigent et al., *The Holy Blood and the Holy Grail,* p. 315.

14. Ibid., p. 359.

15. Ibid., p. 329.

16. Barbara Thiering, *Jesus the Man* (Sydney, Australia: Doubleday, 1992), p. 117.

17. Baigent et al., *The Holy Blood and the Holy Grail,* p. 423.

18. Ibid., p. 430.

19. Ibid., p. 435.

1. *(Left)* Louis de Wohl, the astrologer used by the British for propaganda against the Nazis. From Ellic Howe, *Urania's Children*, William Kimber & Co.

2. *(Below)* The SS-sponsored facsimile edition of Nostradamus's prophecies compiled by Karl Krafft in 1940 and used by the Germans for psychological warfare. From Ellic Howe, *Urania's Children*, William Kimber & Co.

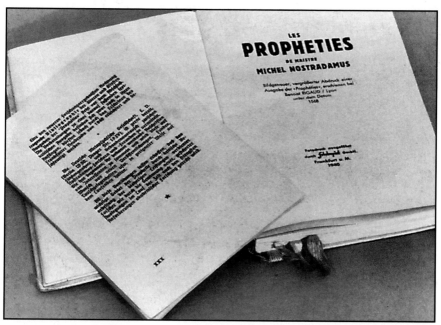

3. *(Top left)* A fake astrological magazine supposedly printed in Germany. It was compiled by British propaganda experts and infiltrated into the Third Reich. From Ellic Howe, *Urania's Children*, William Kimber & Co.

4. *(Bottom left)* Hitler and his deputy Rudolf Hess at a Nazi rally. Evidence shows they may have relied on astrological data to fix the date for Hess's ill-fated flight to Britain. Reprinted by permission of Mirror Australian Telegraph Publications.

5. *(Top right)* Occultists claim the swastika chosen by Hitler is the left-handed version—an evocation of evil and black magic—but is this just another myth? (See chapter 12.) Reprinted by permission of Mirror Australian Telegraph Publications.

6. *(Bottom right)* Hitler was infatuated with his niece, Geli Raubal. Geli shot herself through the heart using his pistol in circumstances eerily similar to the suicide of Stalin's wife. (See chapter 15.) Reprinted by permission of Mirror Australian Telegraph Publications.

Der Führer und Oberste Befehlshaber der Wehrmacht
am 7. November 1935 aus Anlaß der Schaffung der neuen Reichskriegsflagge

L. Geli Raubal, about 1930

7. *(Right)* Trevor Ravenscroft, circa 1972, at the time of publication of his book *The Spear of Destiny*. Courtesy Shirley Griffin.

8. *(Below)* Pencil and watercolor drawing of the Karlskirche, Vienna, by the young Hitler shows him to have been a competent painter. His works are distinguished by an almost total lack of people and animals. (See chapter 2.)

10

Hitler and Providence

The French front, 1917 . . .

Corporal Hitler is asleep in a trench. His dream becomes a nightmare: he is being buried under a pile of melting snow and ice. Unable to breathe, he can feel blood on his chest. He is suddenly awake and trembling. . . .

For once it is quiet on the Western front. Even so, anyone who ventures from the trenches runs the risk of death from a sniper. Despite this Hitler feels the nightmare is a warning to him to get clear of the trench, to flee.

Fully awake now, he throws back his blankets, scrambles clear of the shelter, climbs the banks of the trench, and, dragging the fresh night air into his lungs, begins running.

Without warning a shock wave throws him to the ground. An Allied shell, mysteriously just the one, has been fired, breaking the silence of the night.

Face down on the ground Hitler realizes that, apart from being winded, he is uninjured. As he picks himself up, he catches his breath, then staggers back to the trench. The shell has done its gruesome damage. The foxhole has received a direct hit. All his comrades have been killed. Hitler looks up at the black sky. He thanks Providence for bringing him the vision that saved him.

The above is based on various versions of the story, most

113

of them meant to show that Hitler was one of those people who are guided by a mysterious inner voice.[1]

What appears to be the original version by Hitler is, as with so many other stories about him, far more prosaic, although just as odd:

> I was eating my dinner in a trench with several comrades. Suddenly a voice seemed to be saying to me "get up and go over there." It was so clear and insistent that I obeyed automatically, as if it had been a military order. I rose at once to my feet and walked twenty meters along the trench carrying my dinner in its tin can with me. Then I sat down to go on eating, my mind being once more at rest. Hardly had I done so when a flash and a deafening report came from the part of the trench I had just left. A stray shell had burst over the group in which I had been sitting, and every member of it was killed.[2]

The only consistency in the two versions of the story is the talk of the mysterious "inner voice."

Hitler did claim openly that he was being driven by an inner voice. This is often seen as a sure sign of psychic awareness.[3] The psychic term for it is *clairauditory*: a voice no one else can hear, that guides and advises its receiver; a voice that comes at any time, often in waking moments but also in dreams or a trance. In general terms, a multitude of messages are delivered, but in particular, the most persistent message involves ordering a certain course of action that must be followed. Joan of Arc was afflicted, or possessed, depending on how you look at it, since "hearing voices" is also a sign of mental illness. In medical terms it is a psychosis and the accompanying symptoms include disorders of thought, delusions, and abnormalities of mood, which are, as we have seen, traits that can be attributed to Hitler even at an early age.

While ruling out some of the more fanciful and grotesque claims, King says the occult was a general source of much of the ideology of Hitler and his followers, both the leaders and rank-

and-file membership.[4] Suster places even greater emphasis on it as a guiding force on Hitler. As well as the mysterious voices, he says, Hitler was up to his neck in occult practices. Suster argues that conventional historians who deny this close relationship do so because they have a rationalist's outlook that can make no sense whatever of what strikes them as being a collection of bizarre lunacies.

> One almost feels in the background the existence of a mad syllogism: occultists never enjoy historical significance; Hitler enjoyed historical significance; therefore Hitler was not an occultist. . . .
>
> If I see Hitler saying and doing all the things which occultists say and do, then I am justified in arguing [that] he was an occultist even though in some cases this is not immediately apparent.[5]

Reading this, one can feel another "mad" syllogism coming on: Initiates are under the control of occult forces and are therefore not responsible for their actions; Hitler was an initiate; therefore, Hitler was not responsible for his actions. Such flawed logic brings us to the central theme of this book: *Hitler was an evil human being and must be held responsible for his actions.* Unorthodox writers who seek to explain that magical forces were behind his actions are denying this basic premise, which must be faced if the full truth about Hitler and the Nazis is to be accepted without justification.

Hitler openly admitted to being guided strongly by two major forces that many would consider occult in origin: Providence and intuition, with the inner voice presumably serving as a joint conduit.

On 15 March 1936 he said in a speech: "I go with the assurance of a sleepwalker on the way Providence dictates." A few months later, he reiterated his belief in Providence and expanded on his version of the essence of his self-proclaimed guiding destiny at the Nuremberg rally when he told a Nazi women's conference: "I believe in Providence and I believe Providence to be just. Therefore, I believe that Providence always rewards the strong, industrious, and the upright." He returned to the theme again in his closing speech to the rally: "For us the truth of a wise old saying can really stand as proven: 'Often the deepest love of Providence toward its creatures is expressed in chastisement. A just providence . . . rewards the strong and expresses its love through chastisement!' "[6] This was Hitler's version of the force that guided him!

Did he see this Providence in wider, occult terms: fate, luck, good fortune, coincidence? We may never know, but the evidence is to the contrary. From early in his ascendancy there were very few people foolish or brave enough to ask Hitler to define his terms. In any case, the terms Hitler used were often a matter of time and mood and the interpretation of others.

The role of Providence and its inner voice is said by some observers to have played a key role in Hitler joining the party that he was to swiftly take over and rejuvenate as the Nazi party.

Hitler attended his first meeting of the New German Workers party on 12 September 1919 which was held as usual in a Munich beer hall. Hitler says of this initial contact that he had been ordered by his army bosses to find out what was behind the party—in other words to spy on it.[7] He noted that some twenty or twenty-five people were present "chiefly from the lower classes." His first impression was that this was just another one of those organizations in which "anyone who was not satisfied with developments and no longer had any confidence in the existing parties felt called upon to found a new party," only to have it vanish silently after a time.

That night he had seen and heard enough by the time the principal speaker had finished and was about to leave when the floor was opened to discussion. He remained. One speaker suggested that the state of Bavaria should separate from Prussia and join Austria. Hitler demanded the floor and argued against the suggestion. As a result the speaker he had attacked "left the hall like a wet poodle" and the audience "listened with astonished faces." At the end of the evening a party official introduced himself and pressed a booklet into Hitler's hand.

At the barracks early next morning Hitler was awakened by the hustle and bustle of mice looking for the breadcrumbs he had scattered for them. It was then that he remembered the booklet he had been given. There was nothing mystical or occult-like in its content. Its author, a member of the party, described how he had "returned to national thinking out of the Babel of Marxist and trade-unionist phrases." It reflected a thought process Hitler had gone through a dozen years before. This sparked his first real interest in the possibilities of the party, although he continued to have serious doubts.

To his surprise, less than a week later he received a postcard saying he had been accepted as a member and should attend the next meeting of the executive committee. Hitler had not applied to join; he described his decision to attend not as the work of Providence or an inner voice but as simple curiosity.[8] Even after the next meeting Hitler says he was still largely unimpressed. He found the organization's aims and procedures terrible. "There was nothing, no program, no leaflet, no printed matter at all, no membership cards, not even a miserable rubber stamp."[9]

Nevertheless, back at barracks he found himself struggling with "the hardest question of my life; should I join or should I decline." Reason could only advise him to decline, but his feelings left him with no rest. "As often as I tried to remember the absurdity of this whole club, my feeling argued for it."[10] The one advantage he could come up with for this "absurd little organization" was that it could be molded, or as Hitler says "put into proper form." After two days of agonized ponderings and reflection, he finally came to the conviction that he had to join the party.

> It was the most decisive resolve of my life. From here there was and could be no turning back. And so I registered as a member of the German Workers Party and received a provisional membership with the number seven.[11]

The main reason for detailing Hitler's version of these events is that it shows us he did not assign a role to Providence or its concomitant inner voice for his taking what he considered to be the most important step of his life. The nearest thing to the occult in all this appears to be some fateful illogicality that helped his thought processes. Fest dismisses even this insubstantial story of Hitler's enrollment as an example of him throwing a bit of dramatic lighting on turning points in his life that only later became apparent as such.[12]

An occultic legend has arisen from the fact that Hitler noted his membership card was number seven, a sacred or lucky number in many of the world's cultures. In fact, his membership number was 555; the party membership list began at 501. The number seven refers to his membership on the party's executive committee.[13]

Coincidentally, under the Hebrew system of numerology Hitler is linked to the number seven through his name: the letters that form "Adolf Hitler" add up to seven. Numerologists differ in the various characteristics they attribute to "seven" personalities. However, they generally include people who have a magnetic influence over others: loners, philosophers—and occultists. The numerical value of the individual letters of Hitler's surname amount to 20. Twenty is, of course, Hitler's date of birth. The coincidence of the two numbers is seen as fateful for the person affected and also as giving such a person harmony with cosmic forces.

Incidentally, under the more popular Chaldean system of numerology, Hitler's numbers add up to (or rather reduce to) the single digit of one. To the layperson the only obvious difference between the two is that different letters are given different number values, H, for example, has a value of 5 (five) under the Hebrew system and 8 (eight) under the Chaldean system. American numerologist Morris C. Goodman says Chaldean "ones" have to play the role of leader and will have little help from others to find themselves. Goodman goes on to say the world looks to "ones" for strength and force of character. To fail it would be to fail their mission in life. Neglecting to live up to one's best self can result in displaying the traits of a dictator. Aggression and dominance then manifest themselves. Selfishness and hauteur come to the fore instead of valor and initiative. One's aim then is diverted from the group aim to an egotistical aim. Therefore, the energy which is produced by the generator of the one's name vibrations should be used for constructive purposes only.[14] It is worth noting that the above extract from Goodman's comments was made in 1945, a time when Hitler was the best-known "1" in the world, and any numerological profile that did not contain these characteristics would have lacked credibility.

As for Hitler's other supposed psychic faculty, an unerring intuition, his success in confrontation diplomacy and his early war triumphs are often quoted to justify the claim. In 1935, when he broke the Treaty of Versailles by starting to rearm and introduce conscription, he ignored the disquiet of his diplomatic and military experts by saying that other signatories to the treaty would not actively object. He was right. The British reacted by issuing a "solemn protest" while the French appealed to the League of Nations but spoke of searching for means of conciliation and the need to dispel tension. This was not the language of men who intended to back up their protests with action.[15] According to conventional historians, had Britain and France stood up to Germany at that time, Hitler would have been quickly vanquished.

When Hitler occupied the Rhineland in 1936, again his generals said he was defying the odds. France will do nothing, said Hitler, and he was once again correct. Then in 1938 he sent his troops into Austria with the promise that the action would not result in a strike against Germany. He went on to occupy Czechoslovakia and yet again the Allies failed to make an issue of his warlike actions. "He achieved his triumphs in the Rhineland, in Austria, and in the Czechoslovak crisis by disregarding the advice of most of Germany's diplomatic and military experts and following his own prophetic intuitions about the course of action that would be taken by his opponents," King insists.[16]

Hitler's immensely successful western offensive was also undertaken against the advice of many of his generals. But, adds King, Hitler trusted in his intuition and again was proved right.[17] Suster also backs Hitler's powers of prediction over the expertise of his generals, adding that he even prophesied the exact date of the entry of his troops into Paris.[18]

According to Wagener, Hitler had come to believe in his intuitive powers at an early stage of his career. Once in a conversation Wagener had argued with him that major decisions could not be based on intuition since human senses could be deceptive. Hitler responded, his eyes glowing: "But I do not receive such perceptions through the human senses at all! If it were that sort of perception, it would be amenable to logical proof. . . . Rather, in such cases, I feel as if I were taking my perception from that superdimensional world Einstein has looked into, not with his eyes or conscious mind, but with his mathematics."[19]

Following some further discussion, Hitler elaborated on what happened when he felt that he was receiving these strange messages: "I have a sensation like an inner vibration, as if I were being touched by an invisible charge." He said that whenever he took notice of the impulse, what he said or did as a result always turned out to be correct. However, whenever he ignored it, almost invariably it turned out later that it would have been right to follow "the inner voice."

Hitler went on to curse the intervention of logic at moments of inspiration, allowing "ourselves to be influenced by others who lack any divine spark—and in the meantime, the chance passes and we hit our heads in exasperation and say 'if only you'd followed your first impulse.' "

In further discussion he argued that Frederick the Great and Napoleon frequently acted according to their inspiration. "I am even convinced that the secret of the greatest successes in history is that they were based not on human logic, but on inspirations of the moment. . . . A military commander who does not dare to bring the conviction of his own good luck along with other considerations, to bear on his decisions remains a procrastinator, or an amateur, who will never lead his armies and his people to historic victories."[20]

Irving[21] offers an explanation that weakens much of the prophetic myth argument behind the claims of Hitler's powers of intuition: the *Forschungsamt,* or German "Research Office." It was set up in 1933 to run wiretapping operations, and by 1935 it had developed an efficient decoding section with 240 crypto-analysts aided by a computer capable of decoding three thousand intercepted foreign messages a month. Irving writes: "In the years of his great diplomatic triumphs it was Hitler's furtive knowledge of foreign reports from Moscow, London, Paris, or Ankara that permitted his dazzling flashes of 'intuition.' "[22]

One example given by Irving concerns the political maneuvering in 1939 over Poland. From the time of Munich until the outbreak of war with Britain, the agency fed wiretap information to Hitler on conversations between the British and French governments and their embassies in Berlin. As a result, he was able to follow on an hourly basis how his enemies were reacting to each Nazi ploy and he rightly deduced by 22 August 1939 that while the Western powers might well formally declare war, they would not actually fight—not at first, that is.[23] This suited Hitler, who had not wanted full-scale hostilities to begin until the following year when, incidentally, his astrological stars showed his destiny would be reaching its peak (see chapter 18).

The only problem with Irving's assertion is, as he himself says, "tragically, the entire. . . . Research Office archives were destroyed in 1945."[24]

Hitler's most public displays of what are seen as his psychic abilities came with his speeches in which he conjured a picture of himself as a German Savior. "The people's need taught me to speak," said Hitler on 30 March 1936 in Cologne.

Some occultists came to explain Hitler's relationship with his audience by claiming he was in fact a "psychic vampire," that is, he seemed to draw more power and energy from an audience than he gave out. Ending what to most people would have been an exhausting speech, he appeared more refreshed and invigorated than when he had started. Somewhere he had learned, consciously or unconsciously, to recharge his batteries by drawing on the psychic life forces of others.[25]

According to some nonorthodox historians, such as King and Suster, Hitler's occult powers began to fade from 1942 on as the fortunes of war turned against him and he stopped making public speeches. Hitler knew that should he continue to appear before audiences, instead of having their energy to offer they would be focusing their unconscious resentments on him. They would not give him a positive charge on which to draw. As a result of his fear to face an audience, his psychic batteries began to run down.

To other observers his withdrawal from the public platform at this time adds to the picture of a tempestuous personality who more often than not made decisions on the run, snatching answers from the air and when it suited him ascribing them to intuition of a superhuman form. Such claims hid his erratic, undisciplined nature. His actions more often than not were based not on a known dogma or creed but on the guiding hand of his own personal providence who spoke to him in words no one else heard.

No better example of this is to be had than when it came to the big picture: Hitler's major prediction in a speech to the September 1936 Nuremberg party rally mentioned earlier was so very wrong: "And as a prophet I can say to you: this Reich has lived only the first days of its youth. It will grow on into the centuries, it will become strong and mighty. The banners shall be borne through the ages by ever new generations of our people."

Notes

1. Based on an article in *Sunday Telegraph,* 13 September 1987, p. 32, which is in turn based on Brian Inglis, *The Unknown Guest.* Also quoted as an unidentified report in the Reader's Digest book *Into the Unknown* (Sydney, Australia, 1982), p. 227; also quoted in Arthur C. Clarke, *World of Strange Powers* (London: Collins, 1984), p. 68.

2. George Ward Price, *I Know These Dictators* (1937), cited by Walter Langer, *The Mind of Adolf Hitler* (New York: Basic Books, 1972), p. 34.

3. For example, Francis King, *Satan and Swastika* (St. Albans, Herts, U.K.: Mayflower Books, 1976), p. 266.

4. Ibid., p. 15.

5. Gerald Suster, *Hitler: The Occult Messiah* (New York: St. Martin's Press, 1981), p. xv.

6. N. H. Baynes, *The Speeches of Adolf Hitler,* vol. 2 (New York: Howard Fertig Inc., 1968), pp. 404–405.

7. Adolf Hitler, *Mein Kampf,* trans. Ralph Manheim (London: Hutchinson, 1974), pp. 198–203.

8. Ibid.

9. Ibid.

10. Ibid.

11. Ibid.

12. Joachim C. Fest, *Hitler* (Hammondsworth, Middlesex, U.K.: Pelican Books edition, 1977), p. 177.

13. Hitler, *Mein Kampf,* p. 203.

14. Morris C. Goodman, *Modern Numerology* (Hollywood, Calif.: Wilshire Book Company, 1945), pp. 118–19.

15. Alan Bullock, *Hitler and Stalin: Parallel Lives* (London: HarperCollins, 1991), p. 579.

16. King, *Satan and Swastika,* p. 267.

17. Ibid.

18. Suster, *Hitler: The Occult Messiah,* p. 158.

19. Otto Wagener, *Hitler: Memoirs of a Confidant,* ed. Henry Ashby Turner, trans. Ruth Hein (New Haven, Conn.: Yale University Press, 1985), p. 151.

20. Ibid., pp. 151–52.

21. David Irving, *The War Path* (London: Michael Joseph, 1978), p. 26.

22. Ibid.

23. Ibid., p. xv.

24. Ibid., p. 26.

25. King, *Satan and Swastika,* pp. 254–60.

11

Secret Societies

Even now unorthodox historians insist that occult-based organizations held sway over Hitler, either directly or indirectly. One example was the Ordo Templi Orientis (OTO), which the controversial magician Aleister Crowley had joined in 1912. Crowley we are told confided to the writer Aldous Huxley when they met in Berlin in 1938 that Hitler was a practicing occultist.[1] The implication was apparently that Hitler was an OTO initiate. As we have seen, the New Templars leader also claimed Hitler as an initiate along with Lenin![2] Crowley also confided that the OTO had helped the Nazis to gain power.[3]

But of most interest to us is the occult-based Thule Society because it did play a role in directing Hitler on his path to destiny, although exactly how much of a role remains open to debate. It is difficult to pinpoint the origins of this group whose badge was a swastika with a sword and wreath. Its name originates from the mythical island of the same name which legend places in the North Atlantic between Scandinavia and Greenland. According to mythology, this area was the original home of the first members of Nordic civilization, blond, blue-eyed vegetarians. Some versions of the myth say that the island had once been part of the lost continent of Atlantis. The Thulists believed they were the descendants of the secret chiefs of this "master race."[4]

The society's twentieth-century ideology was influenced by the likes of Liebenfels, who we have already met,[5] and members of the German Order Walvater of the Holy Grail, one of a number of secret and murky racist groups that came into existence prior to World War I. Leading German Order members were deeply involved in occult ideology including its first head, Hermann Pohl, a renegade Freemason who sold copper rings with runic inscriptions that he claimed possessed magical qualities and would guard their owners from material and spiritual dangers.[6]

The reference in its name to the Holy Grail is interesting in the light of Hitler's passion for Parsifal, yet it does not appear to have been explored by either occult or conventional historians. On the other hand, it may be that the "Holy Grail" part of the name was more symbolic than meaningful; certainly there is a lack of a more substantial evidence to speculate further.

Some historians say that the Thule Society started as no more than a political study group, although at one point it seems to have adopted the German Order's Freemasonlike initiation ritual, which ended with new initiates being told they were now above inferior racial elements such as the Jews.[7]

If it were originally only a study group, at some stage late in World War I it underwent some fundamental changes in status and influence to emerge as a powerful force with very definite aims within the community. It could claim many members from the upper echelon of Bavarian society.

From the middle of 1918 the distinction between the German Order Walvater and the Thule Society in Bavaria became blurred, indeed "there is some evidence that they formally amalgamated by early 1919."[8]

Thule meetings became gatherings of many local dignitaries—judges, lawyers, aristocrats, doctors, university lecturers, scientists, military officers, industrialists, and businessmen fearful at the inroads the Communists were making in the turmoil of post-war Germany. Its members included Franz Gurtner, the Bavarian Minister of Justice who was to hold the same position in the Nazi regime; Pohner, the police commissioner of Munich (when Pohner was asked if he was aware of the existence of right-wing murder squads in Bavaria, he responded "yes, but not enough of them"[9]); and Wilhelm Frick, the assistant police chief who became the Minister of the Interior in the Third Reich.

The outspoken Pohner induced the Munich police not to interfere with Hitler's *Putsch* (coup) of 8 November 1923, and went on trial with Hitler and others involved during which he declared "for five years I did nothing but high treason." He was convicted and sentenced to several months' imprisonment. Although he became disillusioned with the Nazis he did not openly break with them. He died in an auto accident shortly after his release from jail. Frick, who also went to jail with the conspirators, became Minister for the Interior in Thuringia in 1930. In that position he tried to obtain German citizenship for Hitler by making him a gendarme in the small Thuringian town of Hildburg-hausen. Hitler dropped the scheme as a result of public ridicule.[10]

In 1919 with the Communist seizure of power in several German cities including Munich, the society is said by a number of sources to have organized a terrorist network that supplied arms to the rightist counterrevolutionaries and distributed German nationalist and anti-Semitic literature. In retaliation the Communist militia raided the society's Munich headquarters and several leading Thulists were taken hostage and shot dead.

However, the most significant action of the Thule Society in terms of world history was in starting the German Workers party, which Hitler reorganized into the Nazi party. The party initially appears to have been an attempt by the largely professional/upper-middle-class Thulists to marshal the workers into an anti-Communist, pro-nationalist alliance. The party was at first a flaccid affair, its members noted for their beer drinking as much as for their politics. On the night of 12 September 1919, Hitler walked into one of their meetings and changed all that.[11] We know, of course, that Hitler was a member of the Workers party, but whether he went on to become a member of the Thule Society is debatable.

One thing that links him to the Thulists is the name of a person he deeply admired, Dietrich Eckart. Eckart was the spiritual founder of the Nazi party,[12] and also, some commentators claim, a member of the Thulists—even of an occult inner circle. Eckart drank heavily and was addicted to morphine; the latter helped him achieve a "transcendent consciousness."[13] Bullock provides another description of the unsavory Eckart: A racist with an enthusiasm for Nordic folklore and a taste for Jew-baiting.[14]

Eckart's violent behavior during bouts of drug withdrawal led him to periods of detention in an asylum, where, using inmates as actors, he staged some of the neo-pagan Germanic plays he had written which had been rejected by outside theaters and producers.[15] Without citing a source for it, Ravenscroft adds the suggestion that one of these plays may even have been about the Holy Lance.[16]

Further evidence of Eckart's instability is provided by King,[17] who says he was the chief disciple of a certain Tarnhari, an occultist who was either mad, fraudulent, or, as he himself claimed, the miraculously born reincarnation of the chief of the ancient Teutonic tribe of the Volsungen.* Tarnhari was also a hater of Jewry and produced a magazine called *Swastika Letter.*

Ravenscroft argues that under Eckart the Nazi party and Hitler plunged into the Thule Society's "world of cosmology and magic."[18] Eckart told his fellow Thulists that his destiny was to prepare the way for the Antichrist who would lead the Aryan race to glory.[19] The moment of recognition (i.e., that Hitler was the

---

*The Volsungen are named in early Scandinavian and east German history. The *Volsunga Saga,* the story of the tribe, was composed probably some time in the twelfth century, although the oldest manuscript dates from c. 1400, according to R. H. Finch, who was senior lecturer in German at the Queen's University, Belfast, when he edited and translated *The Saga of the Volsungs* (London: Nelson, 1965). Finch comments the saga deals with semihistorical or legendary events and personages of Scandinavian history. "These sagas are often termed Romantic and if one of the characteristics of Romanticism is a nostalgic looking back to the glories of a distant and largely imaginary past, then to that extent at least (it deserves) the epithet." Volsung, the founder of the tribe, appears in some references as the son of the deity Odin of Northern mythology. Finch observes the name *Volsung* may be linked with *Volsi. Volsi* probably means "phallus" and there are in fact definite traces of fertility cult in one version of the saga, the professor adds.

Antichrist) came for Eckart when Hitler declared Providence had spared him from death in World War I so he might claim the Holy Lance to fulfill a world historic destiny.[20]

The most outlandish claims linking Hitler, Eckart, and the Thulists come, as usual, from Ravenscroft: Eckart's final deed before he died in December 1923 was to initiate Hitler "in a monstrous sadistic magic ritual" similar to the rituals performed by Landulf II at Kalot Enbolot in the ninth century.* A description of the ritual under the direction of Eckart and amid participating members of the innermost circle of the Thulists would be "barely comprehensible, let alone credible without some knowledge of the history and practices of ritual magic."[21]

The atrocities which formed part of the ritual were indescribably sadistic and ghastly: many times more horrible than the treatment given those who attempted to murder Hitler.[22] (These would-be assassins of Hitler were slowly strangled by piano wires suspended from butcher's hooks in a Berlin abattoir.) Here is where King parts company with Ravenscroft's attempts to link Hitler inextricably with the so-called inner workings of the Thule Society. King says Ravenscroft does not describe the "monstrous sadistic magic ritual" not because he found it "indescribably sadistic and ghastly" but because there is no evidence whatsoever that any such ritual ever took place—an even better reason for Ravenscroft's silence.[23] King also casts doubts on Eckart's membership in the Thule Society as such by saying it would seem he was never actually a formal member.[24] And further doubts about Hitler being a member of the society arise from Schwaab's findings. He concludes that not only was Hitler never a member, he actually kept his distance from the organization.[25]

---

*Described by Ravenscroft as "the most evil figure of the 9th Century," Landulf II of Capua was named as "Third Man in the Kingdom" by the emperor Louis II. He ruled a territory which stretched from Naples to Calabria. Through his Islamic connections he was able to maintain a castle eyrie in Arab-occupied Sicily called Kalot Enbolot (or Carlta Belota) where he carried out horrific and perverse practices which earned him the reputation as the most feared black magician in the world and eventual excommunication in A.D. 875.

Member or not, there is conventional evidence to show that Hitler felt he owed a debt of gratitude to the mad Eckart. On the very last page of *Mein Kampf* Hitler pays Eckart an extraordinary tribute. Beginning with a mention of "the sixteen heroes"— the men who fell in the Munich *Putsch*—who "sacrificed themselves for us all," Hitler goes on: "And among them I want also to count that man, one of the best who devoted his life to the awakening of his, our people, in his writings and his thoughts and finally his deeds: Dietrich Eckart."[26] It is doubtful whether any other man received such unstinting praise from Hitler.

When Hitler bought and lavishly renovated the Barlow Palace on Briennerstrasse in Munich as that city's headquarters for the Nazis, two prominent busts were installed in what was known as the "senate room": one of Otto von Bismarck, the other of Dietrich Eckart.[27] In the building's canteen a special seat was reserved for Hitler under a portrait of Eckart. "It is a heartbreaking grief to me that Dietrich Eckart did not live to see the party's rise," Hitler said.[28]

So what was really behind the relationship between the two men that caused such grief at its ending? Alan Bullock points out that Eckart, who talked well even when he was fuddled with drink, lent Hitler books, corrected his style in speaking and writing, and at the same time promoted him as the coming savior of Germany.[29] Joachim Fest says Hitler was indebted to Eckart for introduction to the influential and monied segments of Bavarian society.[30] Eckart played a major role in saving Hitler in the party crisis of 1921. The crisis erupted when some members of the executive committee became involved in talks with other right-wing socialist parties and splinter groups aimed at creating a mass party. Hitler was against this from the start; he wanted nothing less than the total submission of the other parties to his rule. In his absence in Berlin, the party leaders continued with the negotiations. This led Hitler to resign on his return to Munich. He gave the executive members an ultimatum: he would only return if offered the position of party chairman with dictatorial powers.

Eckart stepped in as mediator and the "crisis was laid to rest."[31] What it amounted to was a total victory for Hitler.

Eckart took over the editorship of the *Volkischer Beobachter* (National Observer), the party newspaper, and began a well-orchestrated campaign to purvey the Hitler myth. On 4 August of that year he wrote of Hitler as a man who was selfless, self-sacrificing, devoted, and sincere, forever purposeful and alert.[32]

In the following year, when Hitler seized guns from an army barracks on the pretext they were to quell a leftist coup, he found himself in trouble with the law and had to hide out. He took refuge with Eckart for several weeks.[33]

Despite all this, Eckart was not in awe of Hitler. He complained before the 1923 *Putsch* of Hitler's delusions of grandeur and his "Messiah" complex.[34] This comment directly contradicts the version of Ravenscroft and others of Eckart's attitude toward Hitler as the messianic Antichrist.

Once again we are faced with contradictions when it comes to evaluating occult influences. Perhaps Eckart stated his real attitude toward Hitler in the Brennessel Cabaret or wine cellar one night in 1919:

> We need a fellow at the head who can stand the sound of a machine gun. The rabble need to get fear into their pants. We can't use an officer, because the people don't respect them any more. The best would be a worker who knows how to talk. . . . He doesn't need much brains, politics is the stupidest business in the world, and every marketwoman in Munich knows more than the people in the Weimar. I'd rather have a vain monkey who can give the Reds a juicy answer and doesn't run away when people begin swinging table legs, than a dozen learned professors. He must be a bachelor, then we'll get the women.[35]

There is no call for a messianic figure in this job description, indeed it lacks any hint of occult skills, is totally pragmatic, unromantic and unadultered, and comes from a man whose heart must have been made of stone. It also appears to answer the question of the level at which the two men were related.

The SS

In 1896, English author M. P. Shiel wrote a story about a group of supermen roaming Europe. They murdered those people whose physical and mental flaws did not fit their concept of the evolution of humanity. Shiel gave his story a title which proved to be prophetic: *The S.S.*[36]

Heinrich Himmler, one of Hitler's henchmen, was very much taken with the idea of leading a secret society, a desire that was to become the catalyst for an organization that grew out of the Nazi party as the party itself had grown from the Thule Society.

Himmler, a chicken farmer by occupation but more like a pedantic schoolteacher in appearance and manner,[37] was at first treated as a nonentity by fellow members of the party, which he joined in 1923. Because of his loyalty it was decided to give him a nominal role. Hitler placed him in charge of a small body of men, the *Schutzstaffel* (SS),* whose task it was to protect Hitler and other party leaders. Under Himmler the SS grew to monstrous proportions to become an organization that was both a fanatical fighting force and the controller of a vast network of slavery and extermination camps.

The first thing Himmler did when he became its head was to persuade Hitler to allow him to increase its numbers. Soon it had grown to a corps of 30,000.[38] But Himmler had just started. His aim was to make the SS an independent body (eventually with its own mountaintop nation). The SS would become the Nazi Praetorian Guard—the biggest and preferably the only secret society in Germany.[39]

By 1933 its membership had risen to 50,000. In April 1934, Himmler completed the takeover of the nation's political police, the Gestapo.[40] In the same year, members of the SS armed squads arrested and executed leaders of the rival group of thugs, the SA, whose brutal excesses had become embarrassing to the Nazis as they sought a veneer of respectability. However, the major reason

---

*Literally, "Elite Security Force"

Hitler unleashed them on the SA was the very real fear that its leaders were planning a coup against him. The victory became known as the Night of the Long Knives. Himmler personally supervised the firing squads.* An inexorable process of expansion in all directions had begun and soon the party also vanished in the mighty SS shadow so that there ceased to be any road to power that bypassed this black-uniformed body.[41]

We are told that while setting up concentration camps where ultimately millions were to be murdered, tortured, and enslaved, Himmler also worked on the occult aspects of the SS organization, drawing inspiration from disparate disciplines, including the Freemasons, the Knights Templars, the Teutonic Knights, the Order of the Garter, and the Fellowship of the Round Table.[42] The SS is also said to have had certain affinities to the Jesuits, an enforced mysticism that Hitler found slightly ludicrous; in 1940, witnessing the pagan Yule celebrations of the elite *SS Leibstandarte,* Hitler commented to an adjutant that this would never take the place of *Silent Night.*[43]

According to Ravenscroft, Himmler was so fascinated by the Holy Lance and undertook such a compulsive study of its history that in 1935 he had an exact replica of it made.[44] It was kept on his desk at the SS Wewelsberg castle resting on a faded red velvet cushion in an ancient-looking leather case—a temporary talisman until Hitler was able to claim the real relic.

Himmler's quarters at the castle were dedicated to the tenth-century Saxon king, Heinrich I—Henry the Fowler—who had stopped the Magyar horse archers from the East and laid the basis for the German confederation that became, under his son Otto I, the Holy Roman Empire.[45] Himmler biographer Peter Padfield finds doubtful the claim of Ravenscroft and other occult writers that Himmler thought himself to be a reincarnation of Heinrich.

---

*Among the SA leaders executed was Ernst Rohm, one of Hitler's oldest friends who had been a key figure in his early success, organizing secret government funds to the fledgling Nazis, introducing Hitler to influential figures, and ensuring the loyalty of the SA. Hitler gave Rohm the option of suicide, which he refused to take.

The SS leader did not believe in reincarnation. However, he saw the connection in the direct transmission of the blood through generations. Himmler did not mind being called "King Heinrich."[46] There is no speculation that Himmler's worship of Heinrich was inspired by Himmler's original chicken farming occupation.

Ravenscroft[47] says that Wewelsberg was built on "the site of the ruins of an ancient but unidentified medieval burg near Paderborn." Padfield identifies Wewelsberg's medieval origins—the stronghold of the bishops of Paderborn—and says it was derelict and neglected rather than a ruin and that Himmler had it converted[48] rather than built afresh. Whatever the state of the castle, the site itself is on a hill overlooking the Westphalian plain and the River Alme just to the east of Teutoburger forest where in A.D. 9 Hermann the Cherusker defeated the occupying Roman army with forces made up of the united Germanic tribes of Westphalia and Hesse. Hermann is not named by Ravenscroft as one of the possessors of the Lance or as having a room dedicated to his reign in the castle.

According to Ravenscroft the "Spear of Destiny" was the "progressive theme of the interior design and symbolic decoration of the whole castle." Each room was designed to personify the lifestyle of every claimant of the lance beginning with Charles the Great in the ninth century until "the collapse of the Old German Empire in 1806 when the ancient and historic weapon was secreted out of Nuremberg and taken to Vienna where it was out of the ambitious clutches of Napoleon Bonaparte" (the latter doubtful claim we have already dealt with in chapter 3). The room for one claimant, Frederick Barbarossa, was always kept locked and reserved for Hitler should he wish to visit the sacred SS sanctuary.[49] It is unlikely Hitler ever visited the castle.

FitzGerald in his chapter on the castle and its Holy Lance theme says all SS members had to take part regularly in various magical ceremonies which Himmler had devised, adding that behind his back he was referred to as the Grand Master of German occultism.[50]

Michael Howard says Wewelsberg had been remodeled on

the castle in the Arthurian myth of the Holy Grail.[51] Padfield also talks of the castle, as the plans for it developed, becoming in Himmler's eyes what Camelot had been to King Arthur and the Knights of the Round Table and Monsalvat to Parsifal and the Knights of the Holy Grail.[52]

The hideously ludicrous nature of the whole project becomes apparent with the attempt to link it to the Camelot legend. The castle's focal point was a great dining hall with an oaken table to seat twelve picked from the senior *Gruppenführers* (group leaders) to become the SS-knights. The walls were adorned with their coats of arms, although there was a problem in that few had come from the background in which family heraldic crests figure, including Himmler. Designs had to be drafted for them. Below the hall there was a circular cellar known as the "realm of the dead" where on death, the knight and his arms were to be burned.[53]

According to Louis Pauwels and Jacques Bergier, the castle was far from the Arthurian/Parsifal tradition. In fact, it became known as the Black Camelot where black magic initiations were held. They were known as "the ceremonies of the stifling air" from the psychic atmosphere in which they took place. At the height of the ritual, a black mass was performed in accordance with the tradition of Satanism.[54] Brennan claims that the castle was the home of a coven of thirteen, not twelve, SS initiates who dressed in black, carried daggers, and wore signet rings of solid silver inscribed with intricate magical sigils (marks or signs). It is obvious this claim is based on the twelve knights to which Padfield refers, since Brennan has each man with a coat of arms and a seat allotted to him at a round table where all would wait for their Grand Master, Himmler, to begin the ministrations. Sometimes they would sit and meditate, but more often, under the personal direction of Himmler, they would engage in magical rituals and spells, and try to contact the "racial soul." On occasions of special solemnity they would sit at the table and evoke the help of satanic entities in their deadly work of black magic.[55]

Even if magical and occult practices were a feature of the

castle, it would appear that the structure was little used as a gathering place. Even Ravenscroft admits that SS leaders and members of the senior ranks went there as a group at most several times a year.[56]

If all accounts are accurate—a castle dedicated to the Holy Lance, to the Holy Knights, and to ancient German heroes, whose occupants submerged themselves in neopagan rites and satanic masses, and plotted mass murder—then we have a monument to the schizophrenic nature of Himmler and his SS. "Never forget," Himmler told a gathering of his SS-führers, "we are a knightly Order."[57] They were, in fact, a terrible mockery of a knightly order. Their symbols were a death's head skull, runes, and the swastika; their deeds were the worst known to humanity.

The SS reached its peak in 1944 with a fighting force that rivalled the regular army, the Waffen SS, of 38 divisions, with a total of 910,000 men.[58] Its other main branch, the 53,000 SS Death's Head division, left a sickening record: 14 million men, women, and children murdered and millions more who had been subjected to slave labor, torture, and other degradations.[59] Some knights! Some deeds!

In the end, Himmler, denounced by Hitler for attempting to negotiate peace with the Allies in the last days of the war, discredited as a general and broken in spirit, attempted to flee from the scene of his ghastly crimes disguised as a member of the military field police. He was recognized and captured by members of a British patrol. After admitting his true identity he killed himself by taking poison.[60] This was slight retribution for a man who we are told by the occultists sought to invoke the German Volkische legends, pagan gods, and the knightly traditions in a base cause of racial purity resulting in the deaths of those millions of innocents.

There is some support for the argument that Hitler, who originally had not intended to allow the SS to develop to the extent it did, was critical of the philosophical direction in which its leaders took it. Bullock writes that Hitler spoke in scornful terms of those of his followers, such as Himmler, who indulged in pagan myths and rites, and his deputy Hess, who was an astrology fanatic.[61] The important fact is that Hitler was never critical of the SS role as practical organizers of slavery, the concentration camps, and the mass exterminations. However, Hitler's criticism, justified or otherwise, would fit in with his attitude toward occult organizations and beliefs as his own powers expanded. By 1933, when he had gained control of the country, intimidation and attacks on occultism and its followers became rampant. At the same time, Hitler thwarted attempts for full-blown terrorist tactics to be used against the churches—a policy enthusiastically advocated by other Nazi leaders. He realized that millions of Germans found comfort in the church and any attempt to outlaw Christianity would be political suicide.[62]

Shops selling occult material were raided and their goods seized, never to be returned. Newspapers that ran astrological and other occult material had trouble getting supplies of paper. In Berlin and elsewhere the police began confiscating booksellers' stocks of astrological literature, apparently on a haphazard basis, and, according to Ellic Howe, were just as liable to seize serious textbooks.[63] Occult societies were purged including the Theosophists, the followers of Rudolf Steiner, the OTO (*Ordo Templi Orientis*), the Hermetic Order of the Golden Dawn, the Order of New Templars, and even the Thule Society! The Templars leader, Lanz von Liebenfels, who supposedly had such a strong impact on the young Hitler, was forbidden to write for public consumption.[64]

Many individual occultists, astrologers, clairvoyants, and the like—in particular those who predicted that Hitler's signs and stars showed he would bring ruin to himself, Germany, and the world—were thrown into jail or sent to concentration camps, where many died.

Some occultists argue that Hitler's attack on their colleagues and their craft was based on the fact that the Führer wanted there to be only one magic force in Germany, his. But there are flaws in the argument: he allowed the largest occult force, the organized church, to continue (he even made God an ally), while banning the Thulists who supposedly held some mystical sway over him. He did not get rid of people close to him—Himmler and Hess—

who were besotted by the occult. Perhaps he felt there just might be something to it, but clearly he could not understand what, even though he believed his thought processes were at such an advanced level his comprehension was all-encompassing. Should Hitler set his mind to any subject he could bring to it an understanding that came from a process superior to logic and human thought. Why, he could take up material rejected by the great Wagner and turn it into an opera!

Ultimately Hitler chose the known (knowledge) over the unknown (the occult), and established religion over mysticism. Addressing the Nazi Party Congress in 1938, Hitler proclaimed:

At the pinnacle of our program stands not mysterious premonitions, but clear knowledge and hence open avowal. But woe if the movement or the state, through the insinuation of obscure mystical elements, should give unclear orders. And it is enough if this lack of clarity is contained merely in words. There is already a danger if orders are given for the setting up of so-called cult places, because this alone will give birth to the necessity subsequently to devise so-called cult games and cult rituals. *Our cult is exclusively cultivation of that which is natural and hence willed by God.*

Notes

1. Michael Howard, *The Occult Conspiracy* (London: Rider, 1989), p. 135.
2. See chapter 7.
3. Howard, *The Occult Conspiracy,* p. 135.
4. J. H. Broggan, *Occult Reich* (Futura, 1974), quoted in Michael FitzGerald, *Storm Troopers of Satan* (London: Robert Hale, 1990), p. 54.
5. See chapter 7.
6. Francis King, *Satan and Swastika* (St. Albans, Herts, U.K.: Mayflower Books, 1976), p. 85.
7. Ibid.
8. Ibid., p. 86.
9. Ibid., p. 123.

10. Footnote in Adolf Hitler, *Mein Kampf,* trans. Ralph Manheim (London: Hutchinson, 1974), p. 333.

11. See chapter 10.

12. Hitler, *Mein Kampf,* p. 627n.

13. Trevor Ravenscroft, *The Spear of Destiny* (York Beach, Me.: Samuel Weiser Inc., 1982), p. 163.

14. Alan Bullock, *Hitler and Stalin: Parallel Lives* (London: HarperCollins, 1991), p. 89.

15. Konrad Heiden, *Hitler: A Biography,* quoted in Ravenscroft, *The Spear of Destiny,* p. 156.

16. Ravenscroft, *The Spear of Destiny,* p. 156.

17. King, *Satan and Swastika,* p. 99.

18. Ravenscroft, *The Spear of Destiny,* p. 92.

19. Ibid.

20. Ibid.

21. Ibid., p. 155.

22. Ibid.

23. King, *Satan and Swastika,* p. 13.

24. Ibid., p. 98.

25. Edleff Schwaab, *Hitler's Mind: A Plunge into Madness* (New York: Praeger, 1992), p. 71.

26. Hitler, *Mein Kampf,* p. 627.

27. Joachim C. Fest, *Hitler* (Hammondsworth, Middlesex, U.K.: Pelican Books edition, 1977), p. 395.

28. Norman Cameron and R. H. Stevens, *Hitler's Table Talk 1941–44* (London: Weidenfeld and Nicholson, 1953), p. 173.

29. Bullock, *Hitler and Stalin,* p. 89.

30. Fest, *Hitler,* p. 249.

31. Ibid., pp. 208–11.

32. Ibid., p. 212.

33. Ibid., p. 255.

34. Ibid., p. 297.

35. Hitler, *Mein Kampf,* p. 627n.

36. Gerald Suster, *Hitler: The Occult Messiah* (New York: St. Martin's Press, 1981), pp. 15–16.

37. Ibid., p. 125.

38. Ibid.

39. Ibid.

40. Bullock, *Hitler and Stalin,* p. 437.

41. Fest, *Hitler,* p. 702.

42. Howard, *The Occult Conspiracy,* p. 131.

43. David Irving, *The War Path* (London: Michael Joseph, 1978), p. 43.

44. Ravenscroft, *The Spear of Destiny,* pp. 308–11.

45. Peter Padfield, *Himmler Reichsfuhrer—SS* (New York: Henry Holt & Company, 1990), p. 249.

46. Ibid.

47. Ravenscroft, *The Spear of Destiny,* p. 309.

48. Padfield, *Himmler Reichsfuhrer—SS,* p. 139.

49. Ravenscroft, *The Spear of Destiny,* pp 308–11.

50. FitzGerald, *Storm Troopers of Satan,* p. 150.

51. Howard, *The Occult Conspiracy,* p. 139.

52. Padfield, *Himmler Reichsfuhrer—SS,* p. 139.

53. Ibid., p. 248.

54. Louis Pauwels and Jacques Bergier, *The Morning of the Magicians,* cited in FitzGerald, *Storm Troopers of Satan,* p. 148.

55. J. H. Brennan, *Occult Reich* (Futura, 1974), cited in FitzGerald, *Storm Troopers of Satan,* p. 148.

56. Ravenscroft, *The Spear of Destiny,* p. 311.

57. Padfield, *Himmler Reichsfuhrer—SS,* p. 139.

58. Bullock, *Hitler and Stalin,* p. 437.

59. Suster, *Hitler: The Occult Messiah,* p. 192.

60. King, *Satan and Swastika,* p. 252.

61. Bullock, *Hitler and Stalin,* p. 430.

62. Howard, *The Occult Conspiracy,* p. 130.

63. Ellic Howe, *Urania's Children* (London: William Kimber, 1967), p. 115.

64. Suster, *Hitler: The Occult Messiah,* p. 137.

12

The Swastika

As we have seen, a satirical magazine which specialized in attacks on Jews and other minority groups may have had the dubious distinction of providing Hitler with his initial idea for the swastika, the symbol which was to gain instant recognition as uniquely that of the Nazi party for probably the rest of time.[1] The magazine was produced in the Austrian town of Linz where Hitler spent some of his youth and where he had his first taste of German nationalism.

The name *swastika* comes from Sanskrit and means "good luck" or "fortune." It has been found on remains as far back as the Neolithic period and among tribes and countries that have no connection with one another and that are far apart: India, Egypt, Greece, Italy, Spain, America, Mexico, Britanny, and Ireland. It was originally a symbol for the sun.[2] Because of its alleged Aryan origins it was taken up by German extremist movements in both Germany and Austria in the 1890s.[3] It was also used on the mastheads of some nationalistic magazines before World War I and spread from them to the *Wandervogel,* the pre-1914 German youth movement whose members were taken with it as a symbol of Aryan manhood. Many *Wandervogels* who served in the army joined the Freikcorp following the war and painted the swastika on their helmets.[4] The right-wing Freikcorp fought with the army in putting down the Communist uprising in Munich in 1919, a brutal action which was accompanied by a series of massacres costing hundreds of lives.[5]

So the swastika had already been "bloodied" in the name of nationalism when a few months after the failed coup Hitler decided his National Socialist (Nazi) party was lacking a symbol and flag and called for suggestions. All the various designs submitted included the swastika in one form or another.[6] The one finally adopted was designed by Dr. Friedrich Krohn, a dentist from Sternberg. King says Krohn was an occultist and longstanding Thulist who had also been initiated into the German Order.[7]

According to Francis King, Hitler insisted on one significant change to Krohn's flag whose swastika was the right-handed version which is traditionally symbolic of good fortune, spiritual evolution, and the triumph of spirit over matter. Hitler replaced it with the left-handed swastika, regarded by occultists as the equivalent of a reversed crucifix, an evocation of evil, spiritual devolution, and black magic.[8]

A problem arises with King's assertion, which boils down to the definition of what are the right-handed and left-handed swastikas. Michael Barsley clearly states: "history will recall that one man, more than any other is *associated with the right-handed Swastika*" (italics added).[9] The accompanying illustration he uses shows "Hitler's emblem" as being the swastika that King calls the *lefthanded* swastika. The other-facing swastika Barsley calls the sinistral (King's right-handed form) and adds that it has been found in southern India where at one time there lived a left-handed sect. This symbol was adopted by Rudyard Kipling and decorated all his books.[10] Suster agrees with King about the handedness and the meanings of the different-facing symbols saying Krohn's was right-handed because it spins clockwise; Hitler reversed it to spin counter-clockwise.[11] Barsley's explanation is that in the right-handed cross the hooks are facing left to right.[12]

What we are dealing with is subjective definition. However, this confusion weakens King's and Suster's assertion regarding the meanings behind the different facing crosses. We can speculate that Hitler had chosen to reverse the cross *because* of the connotations of black magic and evil in Krohn's cross and *for* the purpose of evoking the positive images of good luck, spiritual evolution, etc., for his fledgling party!

Had Hitler reversed them at all? Hitler, in fact, makes no mention of the direction the swastika is taking or of redesigning it to face the other way, even though he tries to take as much credit as possible for the final design. Such a major change as reversing the swastika would surely have drawn him to comment for the sake of increasing his singular claim to the design without any need to talk of the symbolic or occult significance of such a move, if any.

Hitler writes that as designs for a symbol came pouring in,

I myself did not want to come out publicly at once with my own design, since it was possible that another should produce one just as good or perhaps even better. Actually a dentist from Starnberg [sic] did deliver a design that was not bad at all [Hitler does not bother to name Krohn], and incidentally, was quite close to my own, *having only one fault* [italics added] that a swastika with curved legs was composed into a white disk. I myself, meanwhile, after innumerable attempts, had laid down a final form; a flag with a red background, a white disk and a black swastika in the middle. After long trials I also found a definite proportion between the size of the flag and the size of the white disk, as well as the shape and thickness of the swastika. And this remained final. . . .

As National Socialists we see our programme in our flag. In *red,* we see the social idea of the movement, in *white,* the nationalistic idea, in the *swastika,* the mission of the struggle for victory of the Aryan man, and by the same token the victory of the idea of creative work, which as such always has been and always will be anti-Semitic.[13]

It is highly likely that during the design stage the swastika was tried in both directions and different angles before Hitler settled both points; the major importance of the decision being—for a man who prided himself on being a thwarted artist of great merit—not some unidentified occultic myth, but rather balance and aesthetic value. Such "apparent trifles can in hundreds of thousands of cases give the first impetus toward interest in the movement," Hitler explains in *Mein Kampf*.[14] In his comments on the Nazi symbol Hitler does not even hint at any awareness of occultic significance.

What Hitler wanted was a symbol as easily identifiable to the masses as the Muslim crescent and the Communist hammer and sickle.[15] The one he chose he turned into a symbol of anti-Semitism. Some Nazi leaders wanted the swastika to replace the Bible on church altars along with a copy of *Mein Kampf*.[16] Hitler rejected the idea. It may have been that he could not see a religious significance in the symbol.

The swastika and the church did play a joint role on one important occasion. Cardinal Innitzer, the Catholic Primate of Austria, ordered churches to hoist swastikas and ring bells to welcome Hitler as he was advancing on Vienna to claim the country for the German Reich.[17]

Joachim Fest, in fact, accuses Hitler of pretending that the swastika flag was his own invention whereas Krohn had designed it for a local party group and in 1919 had recommended its use as the "symbol of national socialist parties." Hitler's own contribution consisted not of the original idea, but of his instant perception of the symbol's psychological magic.[18] That is "psychological," not "occult" magic.

Notes

1. Chapter 1, p. 29.
2. Michael Barsley, *The Left-Handed Book* (London: Souvenir Press, 1966), pp. 118–19.
3. Adolf Hitler, *Mein Kampf*, trans. Ralph Manheim (London: Hutchinson, 1974), p. 451n.
4. Francis King, *Satan and Swastika* (St. Albans, Herts, U.K.: Mayflower Books, 1976), p. 116.
5. Alan Bullock, *Hitler and Stalin: Parallel Lives* (London: HarperCollins, 1991), p. 77.

6. King, *Satan and Swastika,* p. 117.

7. Ibid. For more on the German Order and the Thulists see chapter 11.

8. Ibid.

9. Barsley, *The Left-Handed Book,* p. 119. Barsley quotes his source as Albert Churchward, *Signs & Symbols of Primordial Man* (London: Allen & Unwin, 1910).

10. Ibid.

11. Gerald Suster, *Hitler: The Occult Messiah* (New York: St. Martin's Press, 1981), p. 98.

12. Barsley, *The Left-Handed Book,* p. 118.

13. Hitler, *Mein Kampf,* pp. 451–52.

14. Ibid., p. 450.

15. King, *Satan and Swastika,* p. 116.

16. Michael Howard, *The Occult Conspiracy* (London: Rider, 1989), p. 130.

17. Gordon Brook-Shepherd, *Anschluss: The Rape of Austria* (London: Macmillan, 1963), p. 201.

18. Joachim C. Fest, *Hitler* (Hammondsworth, Middlesex, U.K.: Pelican Books, 1977), p. 193.

13

Anschluss and the Lance

On 14 March 1938, shortly after five o'clock in the afternoon, Hitler arrived in Vienna to complete the annexation of Austria by the Third Reich. Wearing a brown overcoat and standing upright in an open car, his left hand holding the top of the windscreen, his right raised in the Nazi salute, he presented what one observer says was a "tense unsmiling figure" as he moved in triumph through the streets.[1]

With his entourage came SS Death's Head squads and yowling members of the Hitler Youth who were let loose on the streets to carry out acts of intimidation and violence against those who were marked as enemies of the Nazis, including the Jewish community. The first wave of arrests were said to number 76,000 while in an administrative purge of the Austrian public service there were 6,000 immediate dismissals from key ministries.[2]

The next morning, in the historical Heldenplatz, more than two hundred thousand Viennese jammed the square* and the surrounding streets to express with hysterical cheers and Nazi salutes their unbridled enthusiasm for Hitler,[3] who took it all in from the balcony of the ancient Hofburg Palace.[4]

Hitler declared the *anschluss* to the enthusiastic mob: "as

_____

*A rueful British army veteran, Reg Herschy, who entered Vienna in 1945 recalled that he found no one who would admit to having been in the square on that day six years before.

147

Führer and Chancellor of the German Nation . . . I can in this hour report before history the conclusion of the greatest aim in my life: the entry of my homeland into the German Reich."[5]

Amid the rapture the concomitant outrageous lawlessness was ignored. Jews, young and old, rich and poor, religious and nonreligious, were ordered out into the streets to scrub anti-Nazi slogans from the pavements. The water given to them to do the job was often mixed with acid, which burned their fingers, and the implement they were given as a cleansing tool was often a toothbrush.[6] There are a number of eyewitness accounts on record of the humiliation, harassment, and brutality inflicted by the Storm Troopers and Hitler Youth on the citizens they rounded up: In Wahring, one of Vienna's wealthier suburbs, Nazis ordered Jewish women to scrub streets on their knees and then stood over them and urinated on their heads. Some Jews were forced to spit in each other's faces[7] while devout Jews were dragged into temples and made to do knee bends and shout "Heil Hitler" in chorus until they collapsed. Others were made to dance on Torah scrolls outside their desecrated synagogues while Orthodox women were forced to remove their wigs, a step akin to stripping naked. As the wigs were burned these women were further made to dance in the street. Other citizens were caught with Jews and dragged off to the stormtroopers' barracks to clean out filthy toilets.[8]

Among those forced into street cleaning were Chief Rabbi Taglich, seventy-five, and former Surgeon-General Pick. The cabaret performer Felix Grunbaum was clubbed to death, as was the director of the Scala Theatre, Rudolf Beer. Jailed were the librarian of the University of Vienna, Solomon Frankfurter; Nobel Prize winner Oscar Lowi; and noted ear surgeon Heinrich von Neuman.[9] Suicides became common and within a month the mass shipping of Jews to concentration camps had begun. Jews were virtually driven from the professions; they even lost the right to sit on park benches or to use elevators.[10]

What happened not only in Vienna but across Austria, as communities competed with one another to become cleansed of

Jews, was a foretaste for Germany of the barbarity that began with *Kristallnacht* later in the year.*

It is difficult to follow Ravenscroft's sole account of the sequence of events of Hitler's time in Vienna: For one thing, Ravenscroft once again fails to mention dates or times. Some of his other details are also confusing. He has Hitler being welcomed by the mass crowds in the Heldenplatz as he stood on a "reviewing stand in front of the Hofburg"[11] when contemporary photos clearly show Hitler to be, as Fest says,[12] on the balcony with the Nazi-saluting mobs before him.

Following the welcome, it appears, from Ravenscroft's account, that Hitler went on to review an assembly of Austrian SS troops before driving "directly to the Imperial Hotel where the most luxurious suite in the city awaited him."[13] One reason Hitler had gone directly to the hotel was that he was "terrified an attempt would be made to kill him."[14] Arrangements for a civic *dinner* (which would then make it night time on the fourteenth) and reception were cancelled.[15] However, contemporary reports say that huge crowds had also gathered at the Imperial and called Hitler again and again to the balcony, to which he responded.[16]

There is an obvious contradiction in this. If Hitler was afraid for his life, why did he arrive in the capital in an open car that passed through milling mobs? Why did he stand unprotected on a balcony of the Hofburg Palace? And why would he emerge a number of times on the hotel balcony in response to the mob below?

There is more. Ravenscroft tells us that Hitler left the hotel "long after midnight" with but one purpose in mind, to claim the Holy Lance.[17] As we have seen, Hitler arrived in Vienna at 5 P.M. on 14 March and the mass welcome in the Heldenplatz took place the next day—the fifteenth. If Ravenscroft has meant us to understand that the rally in the square he speaks of was on the fifteenth, then there is a further problem: Hitler stayed

---

*It took Austria until 1988 to commemorate the horror that befell the Jews. In that year a monument was unveiled in Vienna. One of its statues depicts an old Jew on hands and knees scrubbing the footpath with a toothbrush.

in Vienna less than twenty-four hours! He was not there on the night of the fifteenth.

After attending a military parade at the Maria-Theresa monument at two o'clock that afternoon—the same parade which Ravenscroft says Hitler attended before going on to the Imperial—Hitler flew out in his Junkers aircraft as the twilight settled on an enervated Vienna.[18]

As the plane headed over the Alps toward Germany, Hitler had only one thing on his mind and it was not an old weapon of doubtful origin. Hitler turned to fellow passenger Wilhelm Keitel, the Wehrmacht Chief of Staff, and showed him a crumpled piece of newspaper which was a sketch map of the Reich's new frontiers showing that Czechoslovakia was now closed in on three sides. Hitler placed his left hand on the map so his forefinger and thumb encompassed Czechoslovakia's frontier. He then winked at Keitel and slowly pinched his finger and thumb together.[19] Clearly if Hitler had ventured abroad it could only have been in the early hours of 15 March.

Ravenscroft says the head of the Nazi occult bureau, SS Colonel Wolfram von Sievers, had arrived in the city a few days before to make sure the lance was not removed by Austrian officials. In doing this he had thrown a cordon of SS Troops around the museum.[20]

In "the early hours" Hitler entered the museum with von Sievers and some other officials including SS head Heinrich Himmler. Once inside he ordered that he be left alone with the symbol that nearly thirty years before he had made the inspiration for his whole life.[21]

> Whatever Hitler's visions on this occasion the scene of the German Führer standing before the ancient weapon must be regarded as the most critical moment of the twentieth century until the Americans claimed the Spear in Nuremburg in 1945.[22]

The allied powers—Britain, France, and Czechoslovakia—had not attempted to stop the annexation of Austria into the Third Reich. However, says Ravenscroft, Churchill—in possession of the

story of the lance and Hitler's belief in its world powers through
Dr. Walter Stein—warned that the Führer's entry into Vienna
constituted a decisive shift in the balance of power and world
war was now inevitable.[23]

If Hitler had ventured out on the only night he spent in Vienna
with but one purpose in mind, his single-mindedness was monu-
mental: The streets were quite obviously unsafe as Carl Zuckmayer,
the German playwright who was in Vienna at the time, wrote,
"the underworld had opened its gates and let loose its lowest, most
revolting, most impure spirits. The city was transformed into a
nightmare painting by Hieronymous Bosch, the air filled with an
incessant, savage, hysterical screeching from male and female
throats . . . in wild hate-filled triumphs."[24] How Hitler would have
slipped unnoticed through such scenes is difficult to imagine, or
to accept. Further, it is obvious Hitler had no need to make the
journey to the museum. With one brief order he could have had
the lance brought to him.

Hitler certainly could have had in mind the Hapsburg Crown
Jewel collection of which the Holy Lance was a small part, but
as booty. The German economy was under severe stress as a result
of Hitler's single-minded preparations for war. Its own gold and
foreign currency reserves were severely depleted. Not surprisingly,
the healthier Austrian gold and currency deposits were withdrawn
to Germany in one of the first acts under *anschluss.* The Hapsburg
collection was sent to Nuremberg, the Nazis' favorite city.[25]

Given all this, plus a dose of commonsense, Ravenscroft's
account of Hitler's reunion with the object in the museum that
allegedly inspired his whole life is hard to take seriously.

The night of 14 March 1938 was one of terror, the first of
many for millions of innocent victims in Europe. It should be
remembered and mourned as such by those who write and study
history, not trivialized or have attention diverted from its dreadful
meaning.

Notes

1. Gordon Brook-Shepherd, *Anschluss: The Rape of Austria* (London: Macmillan, 1963), pp. 199–200.

2. Ibid., p. 198.

3. Ibid., p. 208.

4. Joachim C. Fest, *Hitler* (Hammondsworth, Middlesex, U.K.: Pelican Books, 1977), p. 815.

5. Brook-Shepherd, *Anschluss,* p. 200.

6. George Berkley, *Vienna and Its Jews* (Cambridge, Mass.: Abt Books, 1988), pp. 259–60.

7. Ibid., p. 259.

8. Fest, *Hitler,* p. 816.

9. Berkley, *Vienna and Its Jews,* p. 260.

10. Ibid., p. 261.

11. Trevor Ravenscroft, *The Spear of Destiny* (York Beach, Me.: Samuel Weiser Inc., 1982), p. 315.

12. See note 4.

13. Ravenscroft, *The Spear of Destiny,* p. 316.

14. Ibid.

15. Ibid.

16. Brook-Shepherd, *Anschluss,* p. 201.

17. Ravenscroft, *The Spear of Destiny,* p. 316.

18. David Irving, *The War Path* (London: Michael Joseph, 1978), p. 87.

19. Ibid., p. 88.

20. Ravenscroft, *The Spear of Destiny,* p. 317.

21. Ibid., p. 318.

22. Ibid.

23. Ibid.

24. Quoted by Alan Bullock, *Hitler and Stalin: Parallel Lives* (London: HarperCollins, 1991), p. 628.

25. Berkley, *Vienna and Its Jews,* p. 262.

14

General Patton
and the Holy Lance

By 1938, says Ravenscroft, Hitler had ensured the lance and other treasures taken from Vienna were back in Nuremberg.[1] Hitler decreed that they should rest in the ancient hall of St. Katherine's Church where the lance had previously been held in the city for nearly four hundred years.[2]

Hitler felt that with the lance safely returned to Germany, the war could begin. However the first Allied bombing raid of Nuremberg damaged part of the church and the lance was hastily moved beneath the Nuremberg fortress to a vault specially built to hold the treasures looted by the Nazis.[3] By mistake, when this vast hoard was again moved toward the end of the war to another hiding place, the lance was left behind.[4]

With the war over, U.S. soldiers who had taken command of Nuremberg came across the underground vault in which the wayward object was lying and took possession of it for their country.[5] The date on which the lance fell into the hands of the Americans was 30 April 1945. A matter of hours later Adolf Hitler committed suicide in his Berlin bunker.[6] The occult symbolism of this claimed coincidence is obvious: the lance had passed on to the next claimant to world power in a line of succession that stretched back into history.

Months later the inheritance was confirmed when, with American soldiers guarding the lance, U.S. warplanes dropped the first atom bombs on Hiroshima and Nagasaki.[7]

Of the American politicians and generals who came to Europe in droves and who visited Nuremberg to see the priceless treasures that the Nazis had stored there from all parts of Europe, only General George Patton showed the least interest in the age-old legend of the lance. He organized two local historians to fill him in on its history.[8]

According to Ravenscroft, the enigmatic Patton had, at the height of the battle in Sicily, taken a break to visit Klingsor's castle at Kalot Enbolot above Monte Castello.[9] Klingsor was the fictitious character from Wagner's *Parsifal* based on Landulf the Second, the evil ninth-century figure of whom, as we have seen, Ravenscroft maintains that Hitler believed himself to be the reincarnation.[10]

Patton did tour the historic sites in Sicily extensively early in 1944. He did not, of course, desert the battle to do so. He visited the ancient castle which in the tenth century was the seat of Roger I, the Norman conqueror of Sicily; the city of Himera, which the Carthaginians destroyed in 405 B.C.E.; and enjoyed an aerial sightseeing tour of Moyta and Erice's Norman castle near Traponi. Klingsor's castle at Kalot Enbolot is not mentioned in the itinerary.

At Himera all that was left of the city was a Greek temple. The visit inspired Patton to write some historic fantasy: it was his belief that the temple "marks the spot where Hasdrubal committed suicide in 397 B.C. and the Greeks built a temple to celebrate the fact, but when the Carthaginians came back they destroyed it."[11]

However, any interest Patton had in the tour spots must have been of secondary importance to what was uppermost in his mind at the time. The leader of the U.S. Seventh Army was in disgrace with the American people because he had slapped a soldier and accused him of cowardice during the Sicilian campaign. With Sicily conquered and his fellow generals deeply involved in plans for the invasion of mainland Europe, Patton was left stewing on the Mediterranean island.[12]

The general began his tour to ease his mind, and was grasping at these straws of the past since the present held nothing for him.

Patton had a "sixth sense" which had come into its own during the war. U.S. General Omar Bradley recalled years later that Patton could foresee situations as they were developing and prepare to deal with them. After crossing the Moselle River near Coblenz with about three divisions and moving rapidly south, Patton suddenly stopped his advance and collected his forces. "Some members of my Twelfth Army group staff expressed surprise and wondered why he did not keep going as the advance was going so well. Knowing Patton's feel for the battle I suggested there must be a reason which George felt but which was not apparent from the information we had. True, the next day he was hit by a strong counterattack which he was able to repel because he had stopped and regrouped."[13]

Frederick Ayer, a nephew of Patton, recalls that he once asked his uncle if he believed in reincarnation.[14] Patton replied:

There has never been any question. I just don't think it, I damn well know there are places I've been before, and not in this life. For instance when I took over my first command in France (in World War I), at Langres, a young French liaison officer offered to show me around since I had never been there before. For some reason I said "You don't have to, I know this place. I know it well." . . . I told the drivers where to go—almost as if someone were at my ear, whispering the directions. I took him to the Roman Amphitheatre, the drill ground, the Forum and the Temples of Mars and Apollo. . . . I even showed him correctly the spot where Caesar had earlier pitched his tent. But I never made a wrong turn. You see I had been there before.[15]

Patton believed he had been a Roman warrior in a previous life.[16]

What is interesting about these revelations of Patton's thought processes regarding his theorizing and/or fantasizing about what took place at the Greek temple site and his sense of "knowing" his way around Langres is that Patton seems to have been in contact with similar transcendental sources for gathering historical material that Ravenscroft claims Stein had uniquely unearthed, that is, use of occult faculties and mind expansion to reveal events in history that are not to be found in written records.[17] Yet Ravenscroft appears to have been unaware that Patton and his mentor shared this remarkable "faculty."

There is a further irony in Patton's role in this story. His nephew says that the general once told him, "A man must know his own destiny, he must know what he was meant to be." Patton went on to say,

> Once, twice, or at the very most, three times, Fate will reach out and tap a man on the shoulder. He usually says, "Go away, I'm busy," or "I don't know you so don't bother me." But if he has the imagination he will turn around and Fate will point out to him what fork in the road he should take. If he has the guts he will take it.[18]

The words demonstrate a belief of Hitler's in an almost uncanny manner. In a lecture to his adjutants in 1938, Hitler said: "There is but one moment when the Goddess of Fortune wafts by and if you don't grasp her by the hem you won't get a second chance."[19]

As for Ravenscroft's claims that Patton took more time off from his military duty, this time to visit the Holy Lance in Nuremberg and learn of its history, at the time the general was supposedly doing so he was up to his neck in yet another controversy. With the war over he had publicly expressed the opinion that the Americans should now be prepared to continue fighting—against their allies the Russians.[20] He had also run into further trouble with actions and words* that showed he disagreed with the policy of uprooting all former Nazis from German society.[21]

---

*Despite the evidence of Nazi atrocities he had witnessed, Patton had begun to regard the Germans not as enemies, but as future allies against Communist Russia. In a letter to his wife following a visit to the devastated Berlin, he wrote: "We have destroyed what could have been a good race and are about to replace them with the Mongolian savages and all Europe with Communism."

Twice cautioned by General Eisenhower, at a press conference he was asked: "Didn't most ordinary Nazis join the party in about the same way that Americans become Republicans or Democrats?" When he replied yes, he unleashed a storm of protest.[22] On 2 October 1945, Eisenhower sacked him as head of the Third Army.[23] It is hard to imagine that anything other than the sacking from the force he had led to such outstanding victories occupied his mind at that time. Neither Ladislas Farago, a Patton biographer, nor Ayer record Patton visiting Nuremberg let alone taking an interest in the Holy Lance.

Patton was badly injured in a car accident on 9 December 1945 and died on the twenty-first of that month.[24]

America returned the lance to Austria, along with the other treasures the Nazis had looted. Today it stands in the Treasure House where Hitler allegedly set eyes on it in 1909.

Notes

1. Trevor Ravenscroft, *The Spear of Destiny* (York Beach, Me.: Samuel Weiser Inc., 1982), p. 330.

2. F. L. Cross, ed., *The Oxford Dictionary of the Christian Church* (London: Oxford University Press, 1958), p. 783.

3. Ravenscroft, *The Spear of Destiny,* p. 333.

4. Ibid., p. 346.

5. Ibid., p. 342.

6. Ibid., p. 324.

7. Ibid., p. 349.

8. Ibid., pp. 348–49.

9. Ibid., p. 349.

10. See chapter 5.

11. Ladislas Farago, *Patton: Ordeal and Triumph* (New York: Ivan Obolensky Inc., 1964), pp. 366–67.

12. Ibid., p. 367.

13. Frederick Ayer, *Before the Colors Fade* (Dunwoody, Ga.: Norman S. Berg, 1971), quoted in unnumbered foreword page.

14. Ibid., p. 95.

15. Ibid.

16. *Into the Unknown* (Sydney: Reader's Digest, 1982), caption, p. 161.

17. See chapter 7.

18. Ayer, *Before the Colors Fade,* p. 101.

19. David Irving, *The War Path* (London: Michael Joseph, 1978), p. xi.

20. Farago, *Patton,* p. 812.

21. John S. Bowman, ed., *Chronicles of Twentieth-Century History* (London: Bison Books, 1989), p. 135.

22. Farago, *Patton,* p. 812.

23. Bowman, *Chronicles of Twentieth-Century History,* p. 135.

24. Ibid.

15

Hitler and Occult Sex

We are told Hitler indulged in occult initiation rites "derived from the horrible sexual magic of Aleister Crowley,"[1] one of the most infamous black magicians of the twentieth century and dubbed by the British Press—with its passion for superlatives—as the "world's wickedest man." However, the two most persistent claims regarding Hitler's sexuality are contradictory and irreconcilable: (1) Hitler had perverted sexual desires, most often involving sado-masochism; (2) Hitler was not interested in sex. The opposing characteristics came to be personified in Geli Raubal, the daughter of Hitler's half-sister, Angela. Angela moved in as housekeeper for him in 1928. Geli was then seventeen and Hitler quickly became fascinated with her[2] despite the fact that there was more than a twenty-year difference in their ages.

The affection Hitler felt for the pretty, superficial niece soon developed into a passionate relationship, "hopelessly burdened by his intolerance, his romantic ideal of womanhood, and avuncular scruples."[3] However, both sides at first felt they benefited from the relationship. Geli enjoyed being with her uncle, especially as his political rise from 1929 to 1931 began to bring him fame.[4] Hitler rather enjoyed the aura of bohemian freedom and the suggestion of a grand and fateful passion in the liaison between uncle and niece.[5]

All that was to change in an outburst of violence. It began

one night when Hitler found out that Geli had made love to his chauffeur, Emil Maurice, the man who was her real lover.[6] Perhaps Geli had come to realize in that moment of anger that she could never have a life of her own. In any case, on 18 September 1931 she shot herself* through the heart using Hitler's own 6.35mm Walther pistol.[7]

Hitler was stunned and completely baffled. No other event in his personal life had affected him as strongly as this. For weeks he seemed close to a nervous breakdown. In his fits of gloom he even spoke of suicide.[8] Hitler turned Geli's room in their Prinzregentstrasse apartment (in Munich) into a shrine and spent hours alone in it.[9] The emotional damage he suffered was never repaired, claims Irving.[10]

Ravenscroft claims that apart from Rauschning[11] the other leading biographers of Hitler fail altogether to understand that a "monstrous sexual perversion was the very core of his whole existence, the source of his mediumistic and clairvoyant powers and the motivation behind every act through which he reaped a sadistic vengence on humanity."[12] He only knew sexual fulfillment through the extremes of sadism and masochism, sexual delight either through inflicting pain on others or from suffering pain himself. In his early days in Vienna Hitler would furtively retire to the red-light district to have himself tied and whipped by any prostitute[13] who was willing to earn a few miserable *hellers.*†

There is some circumstantial evidence in support of these claims of perversion: Bromberg claims that the only way Hitler could get full sexual satisfaction was to watch a young woman as she

---

*Just over a year after Geli's death, on the evening of 8 November 1932, Stalin's wife, Nadezhda Alliluyeva, argued with him at a Kremlin party and walked out. At thirty-one, Nadezhda was, like Geli with Hitler, twenty years younger than Stalin and attempting to make a life of her own. Much to her husband's displeasure, she had enrolled as a chemistry student at Moscow's Industrial Academy and travelled to and from the Kremlin by public transport. This assertion of her independence only added to the already longstanding yet strained personal relations between the two. That night she committed suicide, like Geli, by shooting herself.

†Old Austrian currency

squatted over his head and urinated or defecated in his face. Bromberg also writes of "an episode of erotogenic masochism involving a young German actress at whose feet Hitler threw himself, asking her to kick him. When she demurred, he pleaded with her to comply with his wish, heaping accusations on himself and grovelling at her feet in such an agonizing manner, that she finally acceded. When she kicked him, he became excited, and as she continued to kick him at his urging, he became increasingly excited." Bromberg adds that the difference in age between Hitler and the young women with whom he had any sexual involvement was usually close to the twenty-three year difference between his parents.[14]

Miller appears to accept without question the authenticity of this account, although similar lurid sex tales, often without the slightest foundation and with only small variations on the above, circulate widely, not only about other dictators, but many well-known persons.

According to Suster, Hitler had another fantasy that involved an image of himself as a Teutonic Knight of the Holy Grail, a man of pure and noble mien. However, there was too much hate in his heart for him to be content merely with the truly pure and noble. There were, for example, "those frightful sexual urges which completely overwhelmed him, and reduced the perfect knight to an abject object, half-crazed with lust, yet unable to summon the words that would bring him satisfaction from a pure Nordic maiden."[15]

Looking inside Hitler's head Suster writes:

> There was a beautiful blonde German woman so superior to his own foul desires, chained to a pillar, completely helpless. Gloating over her was a fat, bald, hook-nosed, perspiring and lascivious Jewish butcher, a monstrous subhuman bent upon defiling the girl's purity. And there was her rescuer, Adolf Hitler, knight of the Grail to whom the woman looked for deliverance. But this hero was only a sham, a coward, a pathetic imitation of a warrior and he could only watch in hopeless despair, helpless and disgraced as the Jewish dragon pawed, clawed, and raped

the German maiden. He would wake up screaming, the Jews *must* be destroyed. It was no use Freud telling him that the Jew of his nightmare was but his own suppressed sexuality.[16]

As far as his niece's role in Hitler's sex life is concerned, some sources claim that the real reason for Geli's death was that she was driven to it as a result of Hitler demanding she commit abnormal sexual acts. While Irving says Hitler jealously guarded Geli, he insists that, contrary to the claims of abnormal sex between them made by Ravenscroft and others, she did not even have normal intimate relations with him.[17] Hitler's sex life in general terms was "quite normal," although in the last ten years of his life his natural libido *was* somewhat diminished: his medical records show only half the usual secretion of testis hormone in his blood, comparable to that of a busy executive or a man serving a long prison sentence.[18]

Apart from not having a sexual relationship with his niece, clinical psychologist Edleff Schwaab doubts that Hitler had sexual contact with Eva Braun, his mistress in later life.[19] This claim is contrary to Ravenscroft's view that it is "common knowledge" Hitler's whole relationship with Braun followed more or less the same sexual pattern as it had with his niece: She suffered his tyranny at all other times except in the bedroom where she became the all-powerful mistress and he the groveling slave.[20]

Despite the conflicting claims of Ravenscroft and Irving, there is a strong presumption that Hitler was incapable of normal sexual relations, whether for physical or psychological reasons, or both.[21] Bullock says Putzi Hanfstaengel, who was one of Hitler's closest companions up to the mid-1930s, maintained that Hitler was impotent and that his "abounding nervous energy" found no normal release. He lived in a sexual no man's land where he only once nearly found a woman who might have given him relief—Geli.[22]

Schwaab concludes that Hitler was neither a sexual satyr nor impotent but a truly asexual male. Schwaab appears to blame this in great part on Hitler's lack of contact with women, which had made him an emotional cripple. As a youth in Vienna he had never experienced "the surprises and acute personal conflicts" of romantic entanglements. His identity as a man was never influenced by any stirring love relationship through which he could have gained a mature understanding of the complexities of human interaction. He was self-absorbed, fearful of intimacy, and showed no signs of having sexual urges. Until the end of his life he never saw beyond a stereotyped image of women.[23]

As for his relationships with women at a social level we find more contradictions from biographers. Hitler was totally disinterested in the companionship of women, says Schwaab.[24] Fest says Hanfstaengel riled some of Hitler's other close followers by his penchant for introducing Hitler to "lovely ladies" of whom Hitler showed little interest.[25] Bullock's somewhat dissenting view is that Hitler was attractive to women and attracted by them; he liked to have beautiful women in his company.[26]

Whatever went on with Hitler's private sex life, his public performances had all the overt erotic arousal of a modern-day pop concert. According to Fest, sound recordings of the period clearly convey the peculiarly obscene, copulatory character of his mass meetings: the silence at the beginning as of a whole multitude holding its breath; the short, shrill yappings, the minor climaxes and first sounds of liberation on the part of the crowd; finally the frenzy, more climaxes, and then the ecstasies released by the finally unblocked oratorical orgasms.[27] The writer Rene Schickele once spoke of Hitler's speeches as being "like sex murder." Many other contemporary observers have tried to describe the sensually charged liquescence of these demonstrations in the language of diabolism.[28]

Hitler may have unconsciously indicated he was aware of such reciprocity when he once called the masses his "only bride." He *may* not marry. He *must* deny himself that joy because he had a bride—Germany. "I am married to the German Volk, to its destiny! I have given my heart, all my thinking and planning, my work, myself!"[29] On the other hand, the comments could be another example of Hitler throwing some retrospective dramatic lighting on turning points in his life, a habit Fest accuses him of.[30]

The strong contradicting assertions noted here, which are being made about Hitler's sexuality to this day, lead to only one certain conclusion: Hitler, the first of history's mass media figures, managed to keep the potentially most revealing aspect of his private life a conjectural mystery, even though his public persona was steeped in sexuality.

Notes

1. Trevor Ravenscroft, *The Spear of Destiny* (York Beach, Me.: Samuel Weiser Inc., 1982), p. 164.

2. Alan Bullock, *Hitler and Stalin: Parallel Lives* (London: HarperCollins, 1991), p. 419.

3. Joachim C. Fest, *Hitler* (Hammondsworth, Middlesex, U.K.: Pelican Books, 1977), p. 351.

4. Bullock, *Hitler and Stalin,* p. 419.

5. Fest, *Hitler,* p. 395.

6. David Irving, *The War Path* (London: Michael Joseph, 1978), p. 109.

7. Ibid.

8. Fest, *Hitler,* p. 478.

9. Irving, *The War Path,* p. 110.

10. Ibid.

11. See chapter 5. Hermann Rauschning was a Nazi renegade who claimed to have had many private conversations with Hitler, although the claim is strongly disputed.

12. Ravenscroft, *The Spear of Destiny,* p. 171.

13. Ibid., p. 173.

14. N. Bromberg, quoted by Alice Miller, *For Your Own Good* (London: Virago Press, 1987), pp. 194–95.

15. Gerald Suster, *Hitler: The Occult Messiah* (New York: St. Martin's Press, 1981), p. 49.

16. Ibid., pp. 49–50.

17. Irving, *The War Path,* p. 109.

18. Ibid., p. 111.

19. Edleff Schwaab, *Hitler's Mind: A Plunge into Madness* (New York: Praeger, 1992), p. 110.

20. Ravenscroft, *The Spear of Destiny,* p. 175.

21. Bullock, *Hitler and Stalin,* p. 421.

22. Ibid.

23. Schwaab, *Hitler's Mind,* p. 111.

24. Ibid., p. 110.

25. Fest, *Hitler,* p. 256.

26. Bullock, *Hitler and Stalin,* p. 419.

27. Fest, *Hitler,* p. 481.

28. Ibid., pp. 481–82.

29. Otto Wagener, *Hitler: Memoirs of a Confidant,* ed. Henry Ashby Turner, trans. Ruth Hein (New Haven, Conn.: Yale University Press, 1985), p. 33.

30. See chapter 10.

16

Why?

In chapter 3 I speculated, albeit briefly, on why Colin Wilson, the distinguished writer on the occult and other mysterious matters, came to praise Ravenscroft's *The Spear of Destiny*. To be fair to him it should be pointed out that the book appears to have drawn similar favorable comment from other reviewers over the years. What most concerns us, however, is how the book has been *perceived* by the reviewers and how they have presented that perception to their readers.

In 1983 the publication *The Atlantean Era* of Ontario, Canada, described Ravenscroft's book as "a journey into mysticism" as well as a "piercingly accurate picture of the mind of Adolf Hitler." The reviewer goes on to say the book is "the factual story of the spear which was used to pierce Christ's side and thus fulfill prophecies from the Scriptures." It asks: "What was this spear that so fascinated Hitler that he spent thirty years discovering its secret and planning how to take possession of it?" The book is "the history of magic, of a struggle for power that forged Germany's destiny . . . an amazing account of the undercurrent of history, the path to initiation and Hitler's secrets."

Book News, the journal of the Spiritual Studies Center of Maryland, asserts in its December 1982 review that the book's "important points have been corroborated by other writers who have addressed the general subject of the occult Reich." It does not name any of the other writers but does admit the story is "highly embellished."

The U.S. Rosicrucian Fellowship journal *Rose Cross* in its review of April 1986 (p. 177) says the book "is one to be read and reread many times by the occult student. . . . Its chilling end will leave the reader in awe of the great work that was done by Christ Jesus." Not only does the book unfold the history of the spear but also discusses the lives of those who lived in the ninth century and were reincarnated in the twentieth century to carry out the debts to humanity that they incurred. As a result of reading it the Rosicrucian reviewer felt "a greater desire to do more for the upliftment of humanity" and hoped it would affect others in the same manner.

The above reviews were supplied to me by Samuel Weiser, the paperback publishers of *The Spear of Destiny* in the United States, with the explanation that they do not have many, as most were "lost in a flood when we moved to Maine from New York."

Few though they are, all show that the one thing all reviewers considered was the question of authenticity, the truth of the story. All concluded it was based on fact and so informed their readers. By this stage most readers of this book will have formed a contrary opinion.

I had raised the question of authenticity with Weiser, in December 1993, which was the main reason I contacted the company. There was no response to my initial letter so a month later I wrote again. The response, which came in February 1994, was terse. To my question "Do you believe the book to be a factual account of events concerning Hitler and his experiences with the Holy Lance?" Vice President B. Lundsted responded: "Do not know."

Of course the authenticity of all books published cannot be guaranteed by their publisher—the Bible is a classic example. But when the subject concerns events of the current century, it seldom is too difficult to carry out sufficient research to raise or dispel doubts, enough for a publisher to add a cautionary note that there may be some problem with the authenticity of the material.

I next asked: "Has the issue of its authenticity been raised, if so could you supply details?" In other words, was I the first person to have done so? The response was no.

I asked if Weiser had confirmed the biographical details on the back cover of the book. Could they enlarge on any aspect of them, particularly Ravenscroft's time as a POW? Again Lundsted responded in the negative.

Asked how many copies of *The Spear of Destiny* Weiser had sold, the reply was: "It was published by major publishers before we took it on. So our figures would not be accurate." I could not follow the logic of this response: I had asked how many copies Weiser had sold, not how many had been sold altogether.

Lundsted was unable to provide me with names and addresses of any friends or relatives of Ravenscroft. I explained I had wanted this information so that I could interview them. I also asked whether a member of their firm would object to being interviewed for TV concerning the book and Mr. Ravenscroft. Again, this drew a negative response—"no interest."

In all, a far from satisfactory response to a straightforward attempt on my part to get to the truth of the matter. Let us then attempt to examine the motives of Ravenscroft himself.

Do we simply dismiss the story of Hitler and the Holy Lance as a myth that originated in the mind of Ravenscroft or Stein, or both, and was subsequently seized upon uncritically by other writers and reviewers who promoted it for various reasons? Among the reasons that spring to mind: the myth reinforces occultism as a powerful force; it serves to excuse the very human nature of Hitler's evilness; it sells books.

If we accept as being true, or even partly true, that the Holy Lance influenced Hitler to the extent claimed, then Hitler was capable of intense transcendental flights of thought which went beyond the realms of logic and intelligence. Could such a man have achieved what he did?

With the odds so against the object on which Hitler allegedly gazed being the lance present at the Crucifixion—assuming there was one—we can only accept that Hitler was deluded and also incapable of understanding that there was neither a spiritual nor material message to be had from the object which, in Ravenscroft's words, "was to change his (Hitler's) whole way of life and set him off on the lonely road to total power."[1]

The question remains as to whether it was Ravenscroft or his mentor, Stein, who indulged in fantasy. Was Stein the fantasizer? Did he convince Ravenscroft that he had a relationship with Hitler of some substance—a claim, as we have seen, few could make—which involved the experiencing of the supernatural and the sharing of insights and confidences? Maybe all Stein is guilty of is passing on some basic details to Ravenscroft who took them at face value then allowed his own imagination to soar, ignoring facts, at times distorting them as we have seen, or justifying the unproven as being proven through an unexplained exercise in consciousness known as "mind expansion."

The metaphysical meanderings in *The Spear of Destiny* would surely have been just as acceptable, to those inclined to accept, without the need for a plot involving the major figure of the twentieth century. Stein and/or Ravenscroft obviously felt otherwise.

However, the failure of the story to stand up to scrutiny weakens the message. As a consequence, the biblical legend of the lance, which has inspired believers for centuries, has been belittled.

Then again, Ravenscroft may have had his own agenda. Did he believe that his duty was to warn the world against a return of the evil as personified by the Nazis and thus chose a dramatic means of doing so? The question is prompted by the intriguing interview Ravenscroft gave on a visit to Australia in 1986.[2]

In it Ravenscroft claims powerful secret groups in the United States, Britain, and all other countries of Europe are behind the ugly faces of neo-Nazism. Ravenscroft intimated that, like the post-World War I cliques, these current Nazis and occultists come from business, the professions, and the mainstream political parties; silent supporters from the middle and upper classes, as were the Thulists who gave Hitler his vehicle on which he rode to power by spawning the Nazi party.[3]

In his interview Ravenscroft linked the rise in neo-Nazism

with another message he appeared anxious to convey: the Apocalypse. He is one of those writers who believes it is nigh.

The famous American seer Edgar Cayce in 1936 forecast the world was to be engulfed in natural disasters late this century.[4] Cayce saw earthquakes breaking up the western part of the United States, the Pacific waters submerging most of Japan, and some kind of a vast upheaval altering northern Europe.[5]

Cayce also saw new societies being created by the chosen survivors on new lands arising from the sea where the legendary continents of Atlantis and Lemur are said to have sunk in another apocalyptic era.[6] From these lands, according to legend, the few survivors moved to Europe and parts of Asia and founded the Aryan race. What the famous American seer appears to be hypothesizing is nothing less than a postapocalyptic return of the Aryan race to its homeland. Much of the Nordic folklore of a super race of Atlanteans from which the Aryan race is descended was eagerly lapped up by Nazi occultists.

Cayce believed the Atlanteans dated back 200,000 years B.C. They were immensely headstrong and commanded powers of extrasensory perception and telepathy. The most alarming part of this is Cayce's apparent implication that Hitler and Stalin were reincarnated Atlanteans.[7]

We have a static theme in this apocalyptic persiflage: the chosen few who survive and begin to build a new civilization which will last for centuries—a thousand-year reign—whose leaders are invariably "Aryan." It is as though the best efforts to eradicate Hitler's hateful claims of the Master Race have been less than successful even in apocalyptic outpourings. Perhaps the belief lies too deeply in the Eurocentric psyche, at times dormant, until surfacing suddenly and violently: God-made or human-made destruction, it makes no difference, the Master Race endures. This belief and the concomitant hatred of the Jews unites Europeans—it is the thing they have most in common.

It may be that the meaning of the legend of the Holy Lance is to be found in the story of the Apocalypse: "And I looked and behold a pale horse: and his name that sat on him was Death [in the form of a Roman centurion], and Hell followed with him."[8]

Notes

1. Trevor Ravenscroft, *The Spear of Destiny* (York Beach, Me.: Samuel Weiser Inc., 1982), p. 6.

2. See also chapter 7.

3. See chapter 11.

4. Herbert B. Greenhouse, *Premonitions: A Leap into the Future* (London: Turnstone Press, 1971), pp. 46–47.

5. Max Hassell, *Prophets Without Honor* (New York: Ace Books, 1971), p. 123.

6. Colin Wilson, *The Occult* (London: Granada Publishing), pp. 215–16.

7. Ibid., p. 216.

8. Revelations 6:8 KJV.

Part Two

Hitler and the Cosmos

17

Astrology

The horoscope of the times does not point to peace but to war.

Adolf Hitler[1]

[To] the circling course of the stars man's affairs and destiny are linked. Flegetanis the heathen saw with his own eyes in the constellations things he was shy to talk about, hidden mysteries.

Wolfram von Eschenbach[2]

Throughout his public life there was an enduring association between Hitler and astrology in the minds of many. A few months before the outbreak of World War II, a Swiss newspaper claimed: "Nobody believes in astrology more than Herr Hitler. The best clients of the International Institute in London are the private astrologers at Berchtesgaden. Every month they ask for new astrological documents. This is because Herr Hitler believes in astrology. And he proves it. . . . Before striking, he chooses the most favorable time indicated by the stars."[3] At the time there was no International Institute in London and no *astrologues particuliers* at Berchtesgaden.[4]

A further report at this time quoting Dr. Nicholas Murray Butler, president of Columbia University, said Hitler had a full-time staff of five astrologers.[5]

Despite these and similar accounts of Hitler's astrological belief, accounts that continued sporadically throughout the war, there appear to be no authenticated records showing that Hitler ever overtly expressed any abiding interest or learned curiosity in astrology, horoscopes, or the like.

One of the most persistent aspects of the astrological-Hitler link is to be found in the still surviving belief he was born under a rare combination of stars that ensured his infamous life. Professional writers Anthony West, a native of New York, and Jan Gerhard Toonder, a Dutchman, say the conjunction of stars at the moment of Hitler's birth is traditionally conceded to generate the most violent qualities of which human nature is capable.[6] The two writers, who have a mutual interest in astrology, drew up a chart for a child born at 6:22 P.M. on 20 April 1889. It shows one of the highlights of its aspects is the relationship of Venus and Mars to Saturn (they are both "square," that is, at an angle of 90 degrees to Saturn). The chart shows Venus, the "ruler" of this horoscope, could scarcely be more seriously afflicted.

> The conjunction (of Venus) to Mars, by itself capable of blending the charm of Venus with the energy of Mars, is turned both sour and violent by their mutual square to Saturn. The Venus-Saturn square is held to bring out the worst and most selfish aspects of any given nature, while the Mars-Saturn square is traditionally conceded to generate the most violent qualities of which human nature is capable.
>
> . . . Needless to say, not all people born with such a configuration turn out to be Hitler, but an astrologer would expect something "Hitlerian" from anyone with such a Venus-Mars-Saturn configuration.[7]

One problem here is that they used the *wrong time* for his birth. The Branau parish register volume nineteen shows Hitler was born at *6:30 P.M.* on 20 April 1889.[8] Werner Maser asserts that there is no substance in the much canvassed view that after 1938 the original entries were tampered with.[9] Howe also agrees on the 6:30 P.M. birth time.[10]

Astrologers say one of the most significant pointers to finding character and a person's future is the relationship of the stars to one another at the *moment* of birth—that is, their angle or aspects. This need to know the minute of birth is considered by most professional astrologers vital for a highly accurate reading.

Over many years horoscopes have been published for Hitler based on times that are not just minutes but hours or even days wide of the mark. Even today wrong birth times are used: FitzGerald in his 1990 book gives Hitler's birth as one hour earlier without quoting a source.[11]

Timing forms an important part in the story of the most famous prediction made about Hitler. The astrologer who in 1923 foresaw Hitler's political destiny was Elsbeth Ebertin. Before going into her story we should look briefly at the significance of astrology in Germany in this period. Up to World War I it was largely regarded as an arcane subject, not for the mass market.[12] In fact it was not until the 1930s that daily and weekly astrological advice-type columns became a regular part of the popular press. Their origins can be traced back to 1930, when the British *Sunday Express* printed an article based on the horoscope of the newly born Princess Margaret. It was done half in jest but the response was so great that the astrologer responsible, R. H. Naylor, was commissioned to write a series. As a result circulation soared and rival newspapers hired their own astrologers. From Britain horoscope columns spread to France, then Germany, and America.[13]

German astrologers such as Ebertin had much earlier seen the lucrative potential of astrology if it could be presented in language that was easily understandable. The vehicle they chose for marketing their material for the masses was not horoscopes in daily or weekly newspapers but specific publications. One estimate has it that between 1926 and 1931—the year when the Nazi clampdown on astrologers began in earnest—more than twenty-five widely circulating astrological annuals were being published as well as dozens of magazines.[14]

So widely accepted did astrology become in those postwar years it is claimed there were more practitioners per square kilometer in Germany than anywhere else in the world. "The German preoccupation with astrology at that time was unparalleled in any other country in Europe or the USA," according to Ellic Howe.[15] Its rapid postwar growth moved pioneering psychologist Carl Jung to predict that it would become a subject of serious academic study.[16]

The trauma of the war had been the obvious catalyst: suffering military, psychological, and economic defeat, Germans were desperately seeking assurances and signs of hope. Faith in the prewar systems and methods had gone. In the stars many sought not only a better personal future for themselves but for their country as well, often believing that portents would soon show the coming of the German Messiah.

Ebertin (born 14 May 1880) was the author of one of the popular astrological annuals. She skillfully rode the wave of astrology's boom, becoming known as a highly skilled practitioner, in fact the first woman in Germany to make a living from it. She had set out in her occult life as a graphologist. However, she had become impressed by astrology's possibilities after her own horoscope had been read.[17]

The first of her many books written in clear, concise terms for the general reader was published during World War I and the first issue of her annual, in the same straightforward language, came out in 1917. It was called *A Glance into the Future*.[18] Early in 1923, as she was preparing the following year's edition, Hitler and his Nazi party were conspicuously active in Bavaria. By coincidence, Ebertin had just begun working on some generalized predictions for people born with their natal Sun in Aries when she received a letter from a woman which contained Hitler's birth date.[19]

Some recent accounts do not mention whether Ebertin's correspondent was an admirer and/or a follower of Hitler, or whether she included his name in her letter. The prediction naturally has more weight without Hitler's name being given as a clue.

The 1924 edition of her book went on sale at the end of

July 1923. In it she wrote a "man of action" born on 20 April 1889 (Hitler's birthday), with the sun in the 29th degree of Aries at the time of his birth, "can expose himself to personal danger by excessively uncautious action and could very likely trigger off an uncontrollable crisis." She went on to say that his constellations show he is to be taken very seriously indeed. "He is destined to play a Führer-role in future battles. It seems the man I have in mind, with this Aryan influence, is destined to *sacrifice himself for the German nation,* also to face up to all circumstances with audacity and courage, even when it is a matter of *life and death,* and to give an impulse, which will burst forth quite suddenly, to a German Freedom Movement. But I will not anticipate destiny. Time will show."[20]

Some writers have picked up on the "führer-role" phrase as though Ebertin had coined it, thereby reinforcing the strength of the prediction. However, by 1920–21 Hitler was being referred to within the Nazi party as *führer* (leader). Its use became gradually more frequent from the end of 1921 and appears to have made its debut in the party newspaper *Volkischer Beobachter* on 7 November of that year.[21] In December 1922 the newspaper "seemed in fact . . . to make the explicit claim Hitler was *the* führer for whom Germany was waiting."[22]

Outside of the small group of fanatical Bavarian Nazis, Hitler's image and reputation at this time, so far as the wider German public took any notice of him at all, was little more than that of a vulgar demagogue capable of drumming up passionate op- position to the government among the Munich mob, but little else.[23] On the other hand, Ebertin was a nationally known and respected figure, so the fact that she had bothered with a person who was neither significant nor respected gave her writing all the more impact.

However, in that Ebertin believed Hitler was under the influence of Aries, the basis for the prediction was flawed. Ebertin had the birth day correct, but not the time and it made all the difference. The minute and hour of birth which is normally noted on European birth certificates had not been included in the letter from the woman which had inspired her to draw the chart.[24] For a start, as we have seen, Hitler was born on a cusp day when the star signs change at noon. Aries' ascendancy is from 21 March to 20 April, on which day it is replaced at midday by the influence of Taurus (21 April to 21 May). Therefore, the position of the stars at the time of birth make Hitler a Taurean (the bull) not an Aries (the ram).

Astrologically speaking, Taureans are said to have great willpower and singleminded purpose. They may be slow starters in life but once they've set their goals they will let almost nothing stop them. It sounds like Hitler. It also sounds like a description which could apply to most of us if we really want something!

People born on a cusp can carry a mix of both signs' characteristics. However, as has already been stressed, astrologers say it is the relationship of the stars to one another at the *moment* of birth (their angle or aspects) that truly defines character. Ebertin did not discover the time of Hitler's birth until well after her predictions had been circulated.

If we are to accept the West and Toonder "reading" as based on reliable data, it would appear that getting a birthchart wrong by eight minutes does not make all that much difference! A birthchart for Hitler at the end of *The Spear of Destiny* shows his birth time at 6:17 P.M. and notes that "being born on the Aries/Taurus cusp [Hitler] is in good company with Stalin and Mussolini and a bevy of dictators. It is probably the strongest, most tyrannical time to be born."[25] In fact, the Russian leader was born on 21 December 1879, which is nowhere near the Aries-Taurus cusp (April 20), and the Italian dictator Mussolini's birth date was 29 July 1883, again a non-cusp day.

In any case, Ebertin was so impressed with her findings she moved to Munich to be close to the exciting developments she had foreseen. She attended Hitler's meetings and even had a brief conversation with him.[26]

Having finally learned of the exact time of his birth, Ebertin used it to draw up another chart and from it prophesied: "It will turn out that recent events will not only give this (Hitler) movement inner strength, but external strength as well, so that it will give a mighty impetus to the pendulum of world history."[27]

Some close friends had shown a copy of her annual to Hitler, who had responded: "What on earth have women and the stars got to do with me?" During the summer of 1923 she had tried to explain personally to a number of Hitler's followers "whom I know personally" that their Führer would have very critical aspects in November (1923).[28]

Her subsequent prediction and much of the earlier one were accepted as being fulfilled when Hitler staged an aborted *putsch* on 9 November of that year, which began in a beer cellar and ended in a march to the center of Munich. Police fired shots to disperse the Nazi marchers and some were killed. Hitler fell over and broke a shoulder and quickly fled the scene.

In February 1924, he and a dozen of his followers were brought to trial. All were found guilty of conspiring to overthrow the German government. On 1 April 1924, they were sentenced to various terms of imprisonment: Hitler was given five years. However, he was released from the Landsberg prison less than nine months later. He had spent his time in prison writing *Mein Kampf.*

From 1924, Hitler's horoscope was rarely mentioned in German astrological periodicals. It had become dangerous, even life threatening to criticize Hitler in any way or to write disparagingly—even objectively—about him and that included his horoscope.

In 1933 probably the last public horoscope of Hitler appeared. It was based on a 5:45 A.M. birth arrived at on the basis of past events in Hitler's life. Published in *Astral Warte,** it expressed a disbelief in Hitler's ability to form a government. A month later, with Hitler having been given the reins of power, the journal had to retract the dangerous remark.[29]

By 1934 public references to Hitler's horoscope ceased altogether, probably as a result of a confidential directive to publishers from the Propaganda Ministry. The veto also applied to the

---

*"Astral Viewpoint"

horoscopes of all the leading Nazis and any kind of astrological speculation on the subject of the Third Reich.[30]

Many Germans, as we have seen, were deeply influenced and impressed by astrologers, who were among the media stars of their day. Jealous Nazis regarded them as rivals in the battle for hearts and minds. One of the most outstanding "stars" was Ebertin, who survived the anti-occult purges. King believes she may have owed her freedom from Gestapo persecution to the protection of Hitler himself, an assumption based on the fact that records of his conversations show he frequently made joking but not unfavorable reference to Ebertin and her "astonishing prophecy."[31]

Her annual ceased publication in 1937, with the cryptic message that it was due to circumstances beyond her control. Shortly after the outbreak of war the London *Evening Standard* of 5 October 1939 noted: "The recent disappearance of Hitler's favorite astrologer Elsbeth Ebertin is reported from Breslau. . . . She has not been seen since the start of the war. She enjoys a big reputation among German astrologers and is said to be one of the few persons who knows the exact hour of Hitler's birth."[32]

Ebertin lived quietly in Freiburg until November 1944 when she was killed in an air raid. Ebertin's son, Reinhold, told the astrology magazine *Kosmobiologie* in 1966 that she had foreseen what was to happen to her because she knew the horoscopes of many people living in the houses around her. But if she had moved she would have caused a panic—an offense that would have had her arrested by the Gestapo. People were saying that so long as she was there, nothing very much could happen to them.[33]

A seemingly unequivocal opinion of Hitler's attitude toward astrology is offered by the woman who was one of his secretaries from 1933 until 1945, Fraulein Christa Schroder:

There were popular rumors that Hitler allowed himself to be guided by astrologers before reaching any important decision. I must confess that I never noticed anything of the kind and the subject was never mentioned in conversation. On the contrary, Hitler refuted this by his firmly held conviction that people born on the same day, at the same place, and at the same hour, in no way had the same fate. From this point of view he thought that twins provided the best evidence. He always vigorously rejected the proposition that the fate of individuals depends upon their stars or constellations.

Nevertheless the prediction made by a Munich fortune-teller (Ebertin) in the very first years of his struggle for power greatly impressed him. It seemed her predictions had fulfilled themselves in every respect. But Hitler only spoke very ironically about this coincidence and considered the whole thing a joke.[34]

If Fraulein Schroder's comments are correct, it would appear to indicate Hitler's knowledge of astrology was, indeed, slight.

In an indirect way Hitler demonstrated his attitude toward the subject in one of his table talks in 1942, where he began by sneering at what he calls the great faith the Anglo-Saxon in particular has in horoscopes. He went on to describe horoscopes as swindles whose significance must not, however, be underestimated.

Just think of the trouble given to the British General Staff by the publication by a well-known astrologer of a horoscope foretelling final victory in this war for Germany. All the newspapers in Britain had to dig out all the false prophecies previously published by this eminent quack and reprint them before public anxiety could be pacified![35]

Hitler went on to make the type of statement that often is found on the lips of archskeptics: "In judging any question connected with superstition it must be remembered that, although an oracle's prophecies may be wrong a hundred times (when they are promptly forgotten), it suffices for one prophecy to be fortuitously confirmed by subsequent events, for it to be believed, cherished, and handed down from generation to generation."[36]

At the time of these comments the "uncontrollable crisis" predicted by Ebertin had been well and truly triggered.

Notes

1. Quoted without a source by Joachim C. Fest, *Hitler* (Hammondsworth, Middlesex, U.K.: Pelican Books, 1977), p. 901.

2. Wolfram von Eschenbach, *Parsifal,* quoted by Michael Baigent, Richard Leigh, and Henry Lincoln, *The Holy Blood and the Holy Grail* (London: Jonathan Cape, 1982), pp. 306–307. Also see chapter 9.

3. *The Gazette de Lausanne,* 5 April 1939, quoted by Ellic Howe, *Urania's Children* (London: William Kimber, 1967), p. 235.

4. Ibid., p. 236.

5. *Daily Mail,* 12 July 1939, quoted by Howe, *Urania's Children,* p. 235.

6. Anthony West and Jan Gerhard Toonder, *The Case for Astrology* (London: Macdonald, 1970), p. 27.

7. Ibid.

8. Werner Maser, *Hitler: Legend, Myth and Reality,* trans. Peter and Betty Ross (New York: Penguin and Harper & Row, 1973), p. 1.

9. Ibid., p. 9.

10. Howe, *Urania's Children,* p. 93.

11. Michael FitzGerald, *Storm Troopers of Satan* (London: Robert Hale, 1990), p. 13.

12. Howe, *Urania's Children,* pp. 78–84.

13. West and Toonder, *The Case for Astrology*, pp. 108–109.

14. Howe, *Urania's Children,* p. 102.

15. Ibid., p. 7.

16. Ibid.

17. Ibid., p. 88.

18. Ibid., pp. 88–90.

19. Ibid., p. 90.

20. Ibid., pp. 90–91.

21. Ian Kershaw, *The Hitler Myth* (Oxford, U.K.: Clarendon Press, 1987), p. 21.

22. Ibid., pp. 22–23.

23. Ibid., p. 23.

24. Howe, *Urania's Children,* p. 90.

25. The birth chart of Adolf Hitler by P. I. Naylor with commentary by Jane Dunn, quoted in Trevor Ravenscroft, *The Spear of Destiny* (York Beach, Me.: Samuel Weiser Inc., 1982).

26. Francis King, *Satan and Swastika* (St. Albans, Herts, U.K.: Mayflower Books, 1976), p. 126.

27. Howe, *Urania's Children,* p. 93.

28. Ibid.

29. Ibid., p. 109.

30. Ibid.

31. King, *Satan and Swastika,* p. 234.

32. Howe, *Urania's Children,* p. 236.

33. Ibid., p. 203

34. Albert Zoller, *Hitler Privat,* quoted in Howe, *Urania's Children,* pp. 236–37.

35. *Hitler's Table Talk 1941–44,* trans. Norman Cameron and R. H. Stevens (London: Weidenfeld and Nicholson, 1953), p. 583.

36. Ibid.

18

De Wohl: The Man Behind the Man Behind Hitler

So seriously were reports of Hitler's belief in astrology taken in London in the early stages of the war that British intelligence went so far as to employ their own astrologer, Louis de Wohl, a refugee from Nazi Germany.[1] As we shall see, the precise terms of de Wohl's employment are arguable.

Of Hungarian descent, de Wohl was born on 24 January 1903, and grew up in Berlin. Quick-witted and intelligent, he worked as a journalist and film scriptwriter. He also wrote a number of novels. De Wohl's interest in astrology was sparked in 1930 when his horoscope was cast: he was fascinated by its findings.[2] American psychic investigator Herbert B. Greenhouse says that de Wohl was actually one of Hitler's astrologers who could foresee that Hitler's end was to be violent. Also, foreseeing his own doom by sticking to his professional integrity and not modifying this foreknowledge in an open prediction, he escaped from Germany in 1935.[3] De Wohl arrived in England as a refugee and was soon once again making a living as an astrologer, building a list of apparently satisfied clients.[4]

De Wohl offered his services to the government in 1940, saying that, according to reliable information given him by a neutral diplomat based in London, Hitler was being astrologically advised by a certain Karl Krafft, a Swiss of German ancestry and a strong National Socialist.[5]

De Wohl had one fact to "prove" his claim about Krafft and also why Hitler should be interested in astrology: the propitious planetary positions for Hitler on the tenth of May 1940, to which Krafft would have drawn Hitler's attention. In his most successful campaign and against the advice of his generals, Hitler launched on that day his *blitzkreig,* which began with the swift conquest of Holland and Belgium and culminated within a month in the fall of France.

Hitler's progressed chart (as opposed to his birth chart) for 10 May displayed a pattern of aspects that, for a believer in astrology, almost guaranteed a successful outcome to any undertaking, however risky.[6] Even if it had been learned that Hitler was not acting on the advice of an astrologer, any astrologer could use the planetary aspects of that day as a singularly impressive example of a man being compelled by his stars to act.[7]

Over the following months de Wohl filed reports to the Directorates of Military and Naval Intelligence on German generals and admirals. Ellic Howe claims nobody in these offices took the reports seriously.[8] As a result it was decided to redeploy de Wohl to furnish "black" propaganda for disseminating through Special Operations Executive (SOE) channels.[9]

Late in 1941 the refugee astrologer was sent on a mission to the United States by SOE, which believed that the Germans were running a successful American operation in which they were planting articles and letters in mass-circulation periodicals such as *American Astrology* predicting the certainty of a German victory.[10]

Howe's unnamed ex-SOE source who gave him details of de Wohl's U.S. tour says it was planned that London would send him black propaganda material, which he would pick up from the New York office of the British intelligence organization. De Wohl would feed this material to the U.S. media in whatever manner he chose. In fact, the source says, there was a flaw in the plan which nobody would admit to: No material was ever sent.[11]

Nevertheless the operation went ahead. Howe says de Wohl

had one coup when the American Federation of Scientific Astrologers accepted his offer to address its national convention in Cleveland, Ohio, in August 1941. De Wohl began by comparing the horoscopes of Hitler and Napoleon. Of Hitler's Russian campaign he forecast disaster, saying it was "the first major action Hitler had undertaken which could not have been countersigned by his astrologers." When asked who those astrologers were, he named Krafft.[12]

According to media reports of the conference, de Wohl also told the delegates the findings of Krafft and Hitler's other astrological advisers were checked by the important Geopolitical Institute in Munich headed by a Professor Karl Haushofer.[13] As well as astrologers the Institute was staffed by experts in history, geography, military strategy, meteorology, and included engineers, economists, and mathematicians.[14] According to de Wohl, the Institute had advised Hitler to invade America using Brazil as a stepping stone. An opportune time for attack was when the two major malefics (the planets of Saturn and Uranus) were in Gemini, the sign that rules the United States. This would occur in the spring of the following year.

Some days after the widely publicized convention President Roosevelt said in a speech that he had come into possession of a secret Nazi map showing how they planned to divide and rule Central and South America. Hitler had to deny such a map existed.[15] If de Wohl's statement followed by the map falling into the hands of the U.S. president was not an example of a successful black propaganda operation, then the coincidence is most interesting.

While saying that de Wohl did appear to have been accepted with great enthusiasm by the scientific astrologers' federation, Howe's source summed up her opinion of his mission by claiming what could have been an excellent piece of psychological warfare turned into a flop. If so neither she nor Howe explain why it went on for months longer than planned.

There may have been several reasons why Howe's informants played down the mission: dislike of the flamboyant Hungarian on Howe's part and/or the SOE; an attempt to keep secret the

full ramifications of the operation, one major reason for this secrecy
being that the Americans would not have appreciated being hood-
winked by the British government to the extent their president
was set up in a "sting." Another reason may have been the character
of de Wohl. Howe himself seems to have taken an instant dislike
to de Wohl when they met in 1943 in an office of the British
Political Warfare Executive. Howe describes his fellow employee
as a "flabby elephant of a man." They had been assigned to concoct
a letter that was above a forgery of Krafft's signature. In it Krafft
was alleged to have informed his correspondent that Germany
would lose the war and Hitler would die a violent death. The
plan was to maneuver the letter into the hands of the Gestapo
so that Krafft would be arrested and Hitler would thereby lose
the services of his invaluable astrologer.[16] Krafft was at that time
(1943) well and truly in jail for making astrological projections
injudiciously. The letter would only have amused the Gestapo who
were responsible for his jailing; Krafft was in no position to write
letters.[17]

A second account of de Wohl's U.S. mission paints a different
picture, that of it being highly successful into which far more time,
effort, and money went than Howe's sources were willing to reveal
or suggest.

Author William Stevenson, who had access to British security
documents for his book *A Man Called Intrepid,* says the mission
went well from the start. De Wohl had been billed as a distinguished
astrological figure and news of his impending visit created great
interest in the media. On his arrival in New York de Wohl told
a press conference that Hitler's horoscope showed the planet
Neptune in the house of death; this was dutifully reported.[18]

Denying de Wohl had any contact whatever with the SOE
office in New York, Howe's source adds that he probably never
knew its address.[19] Stevenson, on the other hand, claims the only
"stars" de Wohl ever consulted were in that office.[20]

The harder evidence of Stevenson shows information *was*
relayed from London and passed on to de Wohl who used it
to good effect. His resulting "prophecies" were validated and an

ever-growing audience became convinced of his supernatural powers. Encouraged, de Wohl started producing a *Stars Foretell* column.[21]

The undercover astrologer was used in one "scam" to destabilize the Vichy government on the isle of Martinique off South America on the outer perimeter of the Caribbean. Under instructions from British intelligence de Wohl wrote in his syndicated column that a prominent Vichy official serving in "some ramshackle tropical island" would shortly go "loopy." A week later a French naval officer who escaped from Martinique to the United States told reporters that the island's governor, Admiral Georges Robert, had gone mad. The island government admitted that the admiral was suffering from sunstroke. The outcome of this incident was that de Wohl's stock rose even higher. It was more than incidental that doubts about the governor's sanity helped destabilize his administration.[22]

Stevenson also claims that de Wohl was told to make the following statement in his column: "Hitler's chief jackal is moving into the house of violence." It was a "prediction" of the assassination of Reinhard Heydrich, the Reich Protector of Czechoslovakia. Shortly after it appeared, Heydrich, on his way to Berlin from Prague, was attacked by a four-man team as his vehicle slowed at a hairpin bend. The team had been trained by and was operating under the direction of the British secret service. Heydrich was killed.[23]

Stevenson reveals why it was not surprising—as Howe claims—that de Wohl was received enthusiastically at the Cleveland convention of the Federation of Scientific Astrologers: the federation was an organization created by the British secret service! The *Cleveland News,* obviously unaware it was dealing with a black propaganda front, gave de Wohl a full-page spread calling him "the distinguished Hungarian astro-philosopher." Its unconsciously ironic banner headline read: "ASTROLOGY HAS TOO MANY QUACKS, HE SAYS." Stories from the convention, at which delegates agreed Hitler's stars were on the wane, were run in newspapers across the United States.[24]

Back in Britain de Wohl faded into the background, doing propaganda work for the government. However, he continued unwaveringly to insist that Krafft was Hitler's favorite and esteemed astrologer. Even for long after the war, de Wohl, despite evidence that was by then emerging to the contrary, continued his assertion that Krafft had had Hitler's ear and that up to the last minute of his life Hitler believed in astrology and the demand from intelligence groups for his (de Wohl's) reports never ceased. "More than once we forestalled some of Hitler's tactically unpredictable moves," de Wohl said in a 1947 interview.[25] His postwar career as a lecturer and author lasted longer and was more lucrative than his work as an agent-astrologer.

In 1947–48 articles about his alleged activities were syndicated in newspapers and periodicals all over the world and he became internationally famous. He subsequently abandoned professional astrology and became a Catholic convert.[26]

De Wohl's death on 5 June 1961 in Lucerne, Switzerland, rated an obituary in the *Times* of London. The newspaper was cautious about his wartime claims to have aided the British war effort, saying that de Wohl believed that as Hitler was addicted to astrology it would be of service to Britain for a knowledgeable astrologer to work out what advice the German leader would be receiving. After he was commissioned in the army, de Wohl provided this information with certain additional prophecies. The article concluded by saying that while this had been the most spectacular aspect of his career it was not his life's work. "He was a prolific author, writing many best-selling novels, a number of which were filmed. He will be remembered best for his historical novels with their stories of the lives of the saints. They were lively and credible, if perhaps somewhat didactic on occasion. *The Quiet Light,* the story of St. Thomas Aquinas, and *The Joyful Beggar,* about St. Francis of Assissi, were two of his best known tales," the *Times* adds.[27] It seems somehow incongruous that a man involved in bluff and black propaganda should end up writing about the lives of saintly persons. In predicting that is what he would be best remembered for, the *Times* proved to be correct.

While his books of the saints can still be found in libraries, his book of his wartime experiences, *The Stars of War and Peace,* published in 1952, is much harder to find.

Hitler's "Favorite" Astrologer

Karl Krafft was born in Basle, Switzerland, in 1900. At school he was particularly talented at math and science and went on to study math at Basle University.

Krafft was not an impressive figure: small, almost gnome-like, with black hair and a sallow complexion. Some said their first impression was that he was a real nonentity, until you caught sight of his piercing eyes, which seemed to emanate power.[28] He had no interest in astrology or the occult until his late teens when his sister, Anneliese, of whom he was very fond, died suddenly. He began attending séances to contact her and this aroused his curiosity about occult matters, including astrology.[29]

He came up with what he considered the original idea of examining astrology on a mathematical basis. Krafft spent long hours in the Basle archives analyzing details of various professionals in order to see if the date and time of their births had affected not only their career choices but heredity, physiology, and psychology. He found, at least to his satisfaction, that there was a definite link between birth and future patterns.[30]

Krafft's findings further aroused his interest in astrology and he set up business in Zurich as an astrological adviser for stock exchange speculators. He also hired himself out to companies to cast horoscopes for potential employees. He prospered, until the Great Depression descended on even prudent Switzerland. It hit him not only financially but also mentally and he was confined to a mental institution for a time.[31]

However, his published findings had aroused considerable interest in Germany which, as we have seen, was deeply hooked on the subject. Krafft was invited to lecture in that country. It meant the chance of a new start for him and he grabbed it with both hands.[32]

Once in Germany, he quickly became a rabid Nazi and produced a number of pamphlets in which he claimed astrological data showed a worldwide Jewish conspiracy against the Aryan race.[33] In 1939, a few days after Britain and France declared war on Germany, Krafft was hired by SS leader Himmler's secret intelligence service, the *Reichsicherheitshauptant* (RSHA).[34] As with de Wohl and British intelligence there seems to be some uncertainty about Krafft's work status and job description.

On 2 November 1939, Krafft came up with a prediction which he disclosed in a note to another member of the RSHA, a Dr. Heinrich Fesel. The doctor was a prominent classical scholar and an astrologer and, says Howe, a reluctant employee of the RSHA engaged in investigating occult matters.[35] Krafft's prediction was that Hitler would be in danger between 7 November and 10 November. In the note to Fesel was the phrase "possibility of an attempt of assassination by the use of explosive material."[36]

The reluctant Fesel was by no means anxious to circulate the document in RSHA headquarters so he kept a discreet silence and "filed" it for the very good reason that, as we have seen,[37] astrological prediction concerning the Führer was strictly taboo.[38]

On 8 November Hitler and other veteran members of the Nazi party attended the traditional annual reunion at the Burgergrau beer hall in Munich where the unsuccessful 1923 *putsch* had begun. Within minutes of Hitler and some other party VIPs making a surprisingly early exit (to catch a train for Berlin) a bomb planted behind the speaker's rostrum exploded. Seven people were killed and sixty-three injured.[39]

Early the following morning, Krafft sent a telegram to Hitler's Deputy, Rudolf Hess, at the Reich Chancellory in Berlin pointing out the prediction he had made to Fesel. Krafft went further, adding that the Führer might still be in danger in the days ahead.[40] Krafft was later to boast that his letter had exploded like a second bomb in the Reich Chancellory.[41]

It appears to be widely accepted by historians that the real bomb may have been deliberately planted and timed to go off as soon as Hitler had departed so Germany could accuse France and Britain of a deliberate murder attempt.[42] There was another benefit: the timing showed Providence had Hitler under some occult-like protection.

In any case, the following day Dr. Fesel was ordered to produce the note Krafft had given him and it was soon in the hands of Hitler.[43] About the same time as Hitler was reading it, the Gestapo was arresting Krafft.[44]

Howe says Krafft was able to satisfy his interrogators that he was not involved in a bomb plot and was even able to convince them of the accuracy of astrological predictions under certain circumstances.[45]

The reason why Krafft should send the note to Hess and not directly to Hitler is the subject of some speculation, especially in view of Hess's subsequent and never fully explained action of flying to Britain. Howe says Krafft never met Hess,[46] although for some years Hess may have been a reader of Krafft's newsletter, which was first printed in 1935.[47] On the other hand, Max Hassell says that Krafft had sent his original prediction to Hess a week before the incident. Hess had at first regarded it as a crank letter until the bomb had gone off, whereupon he had come to accept Krafft as a true prophet.[48] If Hassell's version is accepted, it would mean, among other things, that Hess knew nothing of a bomb plot, which would not be surprising as it appears he was very much on the outs with Hitler by this time.[49] Given his well-known belief in astrology and Howe's assertion that he had known of Krafft's writings through his (Krafft's) newsletter, it is unlikely Hess would have simply dismissed the letter as the work of a crank without making some inquiries. Hassell goes on to say that following Krafft's arrest, Hess put pressure on Gestapo chief Himmler to release his newfound prophet.[50]

In any case, whatever the forces at work—be it Hess, Krafft's ability to convince his interrogators of astrology's efficacy, or even occult influences—Krafft was free within a matter of weeks. Krafft did return to work for the RSHA but, Hassell says, in truth his real job was as private astrologer to Hess.[51]

In an address to his generals on 23 November 1939, Hitler

drew attention to the beer hall explosion, inferring his status in the eyes of Providence by saying "in all modesty" he was irreplaceable. Hitler went on to say that the assassination attempt of 8 November "may be repeated."[52] Was Krafft's warning of a further attempt behind those sentiments?

Following Hess's bizarre mission to Britain, Krafft was again arrested—on 12 June 1941—and questioned about his links with Hess. Other astrologers were also interrogated about what they might know of a Krafft-Hess relationship.[53] At this time Krafft was also in trouble with the Gestapo for making another foolish announcement about one of his predictions: Germany would shortly invade the Soviet Union—details of the invasion which began on 22 June 1941 had naturally been Germany's top secret.[54]

This time Krafft spent a year in prison before once again being released without explanation[55]—and without Hess there to protect him!

He was put to work drawing up horoscopes and working on fake Nostradamus predictions. Howe says that some of the papers he had seen after World War II allegedly written by Krafft at this time represent "such futile examples of short essays or background notes obviously written for psychological warfare purposes that one can only wonder at the stupidity of the people who used Krafft's services for this purpose."[56] The reason for his erratic work may lie in the fact that by 1943 Krafft was prophesying Germany's defeat at private meetings of astrologers. This was treason.[57] For a third time the Gestapo dragged him away.

Krafft was held in Oranienburg concentration camp awaiting a trial that never came. In 1944, suffering with typhus and little more than a skeleton, he was packed in a cattle truck for transfer to Buchenwald concentration camp for extermination. He died en route,[58] an end he had not predicted for himself and leaving the way clear for de Wohl to travel the postwar world lecture circuit explaining how he had matched wits with "Hitler's favorite astrologer." In fact, "Hitler's favorite astrologer" never met the Führer, nor worked directly for him.

Notes

1. Francis King, *Satan and Swastika* (St. Albans, Herts, U.K.: Mayflower Books, 1976), p. 11.

2. Ellic Howe, *Urania's Children* (London: William Kimber, 1967), p. 205.

3. Herbert B. Greenhouse, *Premonitions: A Leap into the Future* (London: Turnstone Press, 1971), p. 114. This claim appears to be unsubstantiated. It could have been promulgated by de Wohl himself for promotion purposes.

4. Howe, *Urania's Children*, p. 206.

5. Ibid., pp. 208–209.

6. King, *Satan and Swastika*, p. 11.

7. Anthony West and Jan Gerhard Toonder, *The Case for Astrology* (London: Macdonald, 1970), p. 111.

8. Howe, *Urania's Children*, pp. 209–10.

9. Ibid., p. 210.

10. Ibid.

11. Ibid., pp. 210–12.

12. Ibid., p. 213.

13. See chapter 20.

14. Howe, *Urania's Children*, p. 213.

15. Ibid., p. 214.

16. Ibid., p. 1.

17. Ibid., p. 2.

18. William Stevenson, *A Man Called Intrepid* (London: Macmillan, 1976), p. 367.

19. Howe, *Urania's Children*, p. 211.

20. Stevenson, *A Man Called Intrepid*, p. 367.

21. Ibid., p. 344.

22. Ibid.

23. Ibid., pp. 368–69.

24. Ibid., pp. 367–68.

25. *Sunday Graphic,* 9 November 1947, quoted in Howe, *Urania's Children*, p. 233.

26. Howe, *Urania's Children*, pp. 233–34, including footnote.

27. *London Times,* 5 June 1961, p. 24.

28. Max Hassell, *Prophets Without Honor* (New York: Ace Books, 1971), pp. 161–62.

29. Howe, *Urania's Children,* pp. 129–30.

30. Hassell, *Prophets Without Honor,* p. 162.

31. Ibid., p. 163.

32. Ibid., pp. 163–64.

33. Ibid., p. 164.

34. King, *Satan and Swastika,* p. 237.

35. Howe, *Urania's Children,* p. 169.

36. Ibid.

37. See chapter 17.

38. Howe, *Urania's Children,* p. 169.

39. Ibid., pp. 169–70.

40. Ibid., p. 170.

41. Ibid.

42. King, *Satan and Swastika,* p. 237.

43. Howe, *Urania's Children,* p. 170.

44. Ibid.

45. Ibid.

46. Ibid., p. 232.

47. Ibid., p. 152.

48. Hassell, *Prophets Without Honor,* pp. 165–66.

49. See chapter 20.

50. Hassell, *Prophets Without Honor,* p. 165.

51. Ibid., p. 166.

52. Joachim C. Fest, *Hitler* (Hammondsworth, Middlesex, U.K.: Pelican Books, 1977), p. 909.

53. Howe, *Urania's Children,* p. 202.

54. Hassell, *Prophets Without Honor,* pp. 167–68.

55. Ibid., p. 168.

56. Howe, *Urania's Children,* p. 227.

57. Hassell, *Prophets Without Honor,* pp. 168–69.

58. Ibid., p. 169.

19

Nostradamus Goes to War

Hitler's supposed astrologer, Karl Krafft, was not the only person poring over Nostradamus's quatrains for ulterior motives during World War II. The sixteenth-century astrologer's works became a pliable propaganda tool in the hands of both the Germans and the Allies.

Nostradamus, born in 1503, is often called the father of astrology. In his time, before science insisted on evidence that stood up to observation and experiment, astrology was regarded not as a superstition but a learned profession. Its proof was its claimed consistency. For example, it maintained that when the conjunctions of the major planets known in the sixteenth century—Mars, Jupiter, and Saturn—occurred, there would be major upheavals in society, wars, famines, civil strife, and the like.[1]

Nostradamus trained as both an astrologer and physician. Court favorite of Catherine de Medici, he was also physician to Charles IX. Born a Christian, he converted to Judaism and studied its mystical tradition, giving us the irony that the Jewish-influenced Nostradamus was readily embraced by the Nazis. Then again, Hitler claimed that he learned more from his enemies than his friends.

Nostradamus's *Centuries,* which contain the 966 prediction quatrains, was first published in 1555, eleven years before his death. Nostradamus was very much a man of his own time, and used the peculiar images and associations of Renaissance symbolism to describe events and persons within his own national and spiritual sphere.[2] What's more, he admitted he had scrambled his quatrains, making "a dog's breakfast" of most efforts to interpret them. The prophet leaps about from one time frame to another with no apparent order or continuity.[3] However, in the centuries following, the quatrains have been interpreted as referring to events up to the end of the world. In each era interpreters have "found" meanings in quatrains that refer to their own age. Up to, during, and following World War II some of the quatrains are said by some modern interpreters to forecast the rise and fall of Hitler.

In particular there are two in which the word "Hister" appears in some interpretations. It is, in fact, said to be an old name for the River Danube, rather than a reference to the German dictator.[4]

The first quatrain reads:

> Liberty shall be recovered,
> A black fierce, villainous, evil man shall occupy it,
> When the ties of his alliance are wrought.
> Venice shall be vexed by Hister.

The second quatrain is even more explicit:

> Beasts wild with hunger will cross the rivers,
> The greater part of the battlefield will be against Hister.
> He will drag the leader in a cage of iron,
> When the child of Germany observes no law.

An American expert on Nostradamus, Erika Cheetham explains that liberty was seized or occupied by an evil (black-hearted and black-haired) man; Venice, along with the rest of Italy, was indeed eventually "vexed" by her former ally. As for the second quatrain, Hitler's troops did cross rivers and other boundaries like ravening beasts even though the majority of countries were against them. The last sentence is unclear but may refer to the German naval blockade of Britain.[5]

In 1940 Nazi Propaganda Minister Goebbels ordered the printing of forged Nostradamus prophecies. Leaflets containing these false prophecies were dropped from German aircraft over France and it is claimed so seriously were they taken that morale in both the French army and among the civilians suffered.[6]

In another propaganda coup, Krafft wrote a book, *How Nostradamus Foresaw the Future,* which twisted the quatrains to show Britain was heading for inevitable defeat.[7]

One example of a Nostradamus prediction Krafft worked on when Germany was planning to invade Britain in 1941 was the hundredth quatrain in the second *Centuries*:

> Dedans les isles si horrible tumulte,
> Bien on n'orra qu'une bellique brigue
> Tant grand sera des predateurs insulte
> U'on se viendra ranger a la grand ligue.

His interpretation: *Les Isles* was Great Britain and *predateurs* were the British, a race of people who rob and pillage. The *tumulte* in Britain would be awful, much worse than anyone could imagine. *Bellique brigue* was interpreted as "total war," that is, in every part of *les isles.* The last two lines predict that as a result of the damage the British pirates inflict on the rest of Europe, the other nations rise against her and put an end to her actions.[8]

The allies must have believed the "Nostradamus Bomb" had an impact because they went to a great deal of trouble to produce one of their own. In a counterattack, Ellic Howe and the refugee astrologer Louis de Wohl[9] worked for a British black propaganda organization on forging a number of booklets containing doctored Nostradamus material. Howe was an expert typographer, de Wohl provided the words.[10] In one booklet *Nostradamus Predicts the Course of the War,* supposedly printed by a reputable German publisher, there was a German translation which says Hister ("Hitler") would carry off more victories than he was capable of handling. Consequently six men would murder him in the night. He would be caught naked and unaware and succumb to their attack.[11]

Altogether the booklet contained fifty forged prophecies and a commentary supposedly written by scholars containing a great deal of subtle anti-Nazi propaganda. They were distributed in occupied and neutral countries together with unfavorable horoscopes of Nazi leaders.[12]

Apart from propaganda, the most obvious cause for misinterpretation of the sixteenth-century seer is when a writer tries to make a quatrain fit a particular era. Other mistakes are caused by wishful thinking and mistranslation or combinations of these factors.

Compare this translation of one of the Hister quatrains with the one already quoted:

> Liberty will not be recovered.
> A bold, black, base-born iniquitous man will occupy it;
> When the material of the bridge is completed,
> The republic of Venice will be annoyed by Hister.[13]

The following is claimed by FitzGerald as "one of the most astonishing quatrains which can only refer to an event during the Second World War."[14]

> The assembly will go out from the castle of Franco,
> The ambassador not satisfied will make a schism;
> Those of the Riviera will be involved,
> And they will deny the entry to the great gulf.[15]

FitzGerald interprets this version by Stewart Robb thus: The Spanish dictator Franco held a meeting with Hitler and the Italian dictator Mussolini in 1941 on the *Riviera*. When the other two asked Franco for permission to pass through Spain to attack the British fortress of Gibraltar, Franco denied them—*deny the entry to the great gulf*.[16]

FitzGerald goes on to say the quatrain is the only mention of the Spanish Fascist leader General Franco. "The odds against the name Franco, a meeting of ambassadors on the Riviera, and the denial of 'the entry to the great gulf' all occurring together by chance are more than one in a million, and this prophecy originates in 1550!" FitzGerald enthuses.[17] However, Jean-Charles de Fontbrune, the son of Max the historian and noted Nostradamus interpreter, says the quatrain refers mainly to Franco being named as head of government at Burgos in 1938, although he does agree with Robb on the final line.[18]

The de Fontbrune version of the quatrain:

> Franco will emerge from a junta in a strong place in Castile.
> The representative who has not pleased will make fa(scism)
> those with (Primo) de Rivera will be with him; they will refuse
> to enter into the great gulf of misfortunes (Germany).

De Fontbrune explains: Primo de Rivera was not a geographical place but the name of another Spanish leader who had united two right-wing parties. Further, Nostradamus, being full of puns and others cryptic word plays, could of course have used Franco as meaning France.[19]

Even when the meanings seem clear, there is the problem with interpretation.

Robb's version:

> An old man with the title of chief will arise, of doddering sense,
> Degenerating in knowledge and arms; head of France feared
> by his sister, the country divided, conceded to gendarmes.[20]

De Fontbrune's version:

> The good sense of an old leader will be rendered stupid,
> Losing the glory of his wisdom and feats of arms;
> The chief of France will be suspected by his sister.
> Then the land will be divided and abandoned to the soldiers.[21]

Both agree that this refers to the aged Marshall Petain signing the armistice with Germany in June 1940.

FitzGerald seizes on the word "gendarme" in the Robb translation as a sign of precognition pointing out there were no gendarmes in the sixteenth century so obviously it had to refer to an event occurring in a later era.[22] De Fontbrune simply calls them "soldiers."[23]

FitzGerald believes the reference to "his sister" refers to a sister-in-law who expressed fears about Petain being too old to be head of France.[24] De Fontbrune says "sister" is a reference to France's Latin sister, Italy.[25]

Just about all the quatrains can be argued in such a manner, so it is not surprising that propaganda interpretations suitably presented and given some scholarly source have a certain credibility.

Dr. Max de Fontbrune's book *The Prophecies of Nostradamus* was banned by the Nazi puppet Vichy government in November 1940. His son, Jean-Charles, says the book, published in 1938, had predicted the German army's advance through Belgium to invade France. However, it went on to predict the eventual defeat of Germany and Hitler's wretched end. The Gestapo confiscated the book from every bookshop in France and even broke up and melted down the type.[26]

Howe points out a certain irony in this: while the Germans were trying to undermine the morale of the French population with culled Nostradamus material, the French themselves were busy banning the seer's material in order not to give offense to the occupying Germans.[27]

It is difficult to evaluate what effect, if any, the "Nostradamus war" had on the populations and the soldiers who were its targets: nobody likes to admit being taken in. However, judging by the fact that millions of copies of Nostradamus's works have been sold since, the reputation of the famous old seer was not tarnished by the misuse of his mangled quatrains—they have, after all, survived many a war they allegedly predicted.

Notes

1. Jean-Charles de Fontbrune, *Countdown to Apocalypse* (London: Hutchinson, 1983), preface by Liz Greene, p. xi.

2. Ibid., p. ix.

3. Ibid., pp. ix–x.

4. Michael FitzGerald, *Storm Troopers of Satan* (London: Robert Hale, 1990), p. 121.

5. Erika Cheetham, *The Prophecies of Nostradamus,* quoted in *Mysteries of the Unexplained* (Hong Kong: Reader's Digest, 1982), pp. 17–18.

6. Max Hassell, *Prophets Without Honor* (New York: Ace Books, 1971), p. 166.

7. Ellic Howe, *Urania's Children* (London: William Kimber, 1967), pp. 190–91.

8. Ibid., p. 190.

9. See chapter 18.

10. Howe, *Urania's Children,* p. 216.

11. Ibid., p. 217.

12. Ibid.

13. Stewart Robb, *Prophecies on World Events by Nostradamus,* quoted in FitzGerald, *Storm Troopers of Satan,* p. 121.

14. FitzGerald, *Storm Troopers of Satan,* p. 120.

15. Stewart Robb, quoted in FitzGerald, *Storm Troopers of Satan,* p. 120.

16. FitzGerald, *Storm Troopers of Satan,* pp. 120–21.

17. Ibid., p. 121.

18. De Fontbrune, *Countdown to Apocalypse,* p. 199.

19. Ibid.

20. FitzGerald, *Storm Troopers of Satan,* p. 126.

21. De Fontbrune, *Countdown to Apocalypse,* p. 229.

22. FitzGerald, *Storm Troopers of Satan,* p. 126.

23. De Fontbrune, *Countdown to Apocalypse,* p. 229.

24. FitzGerald, *Storm Troopers of Satan,* p. 126.

25. De Fontbrune, *Countdown to Apocalypse,* p. 229.

26. Ibid., p. xix.

27. Howe, *Urania's Children,* p. 186.

20

Hess: Hitler and His Deputy

The flight of Hitler's deputy, Rudolf Hess, to Britain is one of the most baffling mysteries of World War II. Before we begin to look for influences of a cosmic nature behind the mission, we must first examine the effect of yet another occultist on Hitler.

Karl Haushofer was born in Bavaria in 1869. He became an army officer but seems to have spent many years living a very unmilitary existence in Asia, including a considerable amount of time in Tibet with the Russian George Ivanovitch Gurdjieff between 1903 and 1908. Gurdjieff in the late 1880s or early 1890s had become a Tibetan lama and claimed he had spent time with members of a super race who divulged their secrets to him.[1] Gurdjieff revealed to Haushofer some of those occult secrets that basically involved developing hidden potentials of humans through meditation, intense concentration, and a raising of one's awareness and keeping it raised permanently.[2] Gerald Suster implies Haushofer years later was to pass on these ancient secrets to Hitler.[3] (Some occult writers, while not going along with master race theories, argue that part of a next stage of evolution will be the ability to maintain what we now consider a heightened state of awareness, such as we occasionally reach in moments of intense alertness, on a permanent basis. It is an argument that can become befogged by those occultists who either start with or lapse into racial prejudice: such a state will be restricted to a particular group or race.)

FitzGerald says the knowledge Haushofer passed on to Hitler was far more explosive: "Haushofer was an accomplished black magician . . . the evil genius who completed the satanic transformation of Hitler into a being of almost supernatural dimensions."[4]

Between 1907 and 1912 Haushofer lived mainly in Japan, where he studied the language and began forming the beliefs he was later to develop into a full-blown treatise: the struggle for a nation's life was little more than a contest for land space.[5]

Suster (and Ravenscroft) claim Haushofer, while in Japan, was also initiated into an esoteric Buddhist society known as the Green Dragon.[6] The initiation process involved a novitiate using only his mental powers to activate the germination process in a seed and bringing about its growth so the blossom appeared in a matter of minutes.

Only two other Europeans had been permitted to join the order, which demanded "oaths of secrecy and obedience of a far more strict and uncompromising nature than similar secret societies in the Western world."[7] Each member of the order is sworn to carry out a mission with the pledge he will commit suicide should he fail.[8] This latter claim fits with Haushofer's fate and it could be argued that, through occult influence, it was a contributing cause in Hitler's suicide.

Haushofer returned to Germany before World War I and studied at the University of Munich where he graduated *summa cum laude* in geography, geology, and history.[9] During the war he served as a general on the Western front, where he demonstrated, like General Patton,[10] strong powers of foresight.[11]

Following the war, Haushofer returned to the theories he had been working on in Japan concerning nations and how they survive, and in refining those theories he created what he considered to be a new science which he called geopolitics. Geopolitics was seen by objective observers[12] as little more than a pseudoscience, a justification for German imperialism: Land in which Germans had settled was German, regions in which German was spoken ought to be German, or, at least for cultural purposes, a German sphere of influence.

In the climate of the time, Haushofer's views appealed to both the academics and the disillusioned ex-servicemen, many of whom were resuming their studies and who flocked to hear him. One of these students was Rudolf Hess.[13] In 1921 Haushofer was appointed Honorary Professor of Political Geography at Munich University.[14] Most occult writers drop the honorific.

Two years later, his student was deeply involved in the failed *putsch* which had been instigated by Hitler. Hess's task had been to detain prominent members of the Bavarian cabinet. Hess sought refuge in Haushofer's home and with the help of the honorary professor escaped to Austria.[15] Returning later, Hess was given a light sentence and joined Hitler in jail. According to Suster,[16] Hess persuaded Haushofer to attend Hitler's trial. As a result Haushofer was deeply impressed by Hitler's magnificent courtroom performance in which he railed against the ability of the judges or any man to pass sentence on him—only Providence could do that, Hitler boasted. Other accounts say Haushofer first met Hitler when he visited Hess in jail following the trial. He brought Hitler reading material and they had occasional conversations.

Suster and others go much further in their claims of what happened between Haushofer and Hitler in the Landsberg jail.[17] Not only did Haushofer teach Hitler geopolitics, but it was here that he imparted the "explosive" black magic knowledge mentioned by FitzGerald. Suster says that from Haushofer Hitler also learned the ability to make predictions, greater self-control, and how to speak in public without becoming exhausted. Further, as a result of Haushofer's teachings, Hitler gave up carrying a riding-whip and also drinking alcohol.

Hitler did give up drinking on a permanent basis but his addiction to the riding crop must have been stronger. In an event that occurred some years after he had allegedly given up his crop Hitler surprised his chauffeur Emil Maurice in the room of his niece, Geli Raubal,[18] and "raised his riding whip in such threatening fury that Maurice saved himself only by leaping out the window."[19]

Ravenscroft makes some of the most bizarre, not to say barely coherent, charges of Haushofer's influence on Hitler: He "sought quite consciously and with malicious intent" to teach Hitler "how to unleash the powers of the Apocalyptic Beast against humanity in an attempt to conquer the world." He initiated Hitler "into *The Secret Doctrines* of which his system of geopolitics was but a 'cunningly pointed exteriorization.' . . . He contributed degrees of initiation . . . which served to expand and metamorphose the 'time organism' . . . in Hitler teaching him to consider the evolution of man in tremendous vistas of time." Finally, Haushofer initiated Hitler "into . . . the part which occult blood rites would play in creating a magical mutation in the Aryan Race which would bring about a new stage of evolution, the birth of the Superman."[20]

A more rational examination can only lead us to conclude that it is unlikely Hitler and Haushofer were even close, certainly not close enough to be involved in occult rites or initiation ceremonies on an esoteric teacher-pupil relationship. As James Douglas-Hamilton[21] points out, the two men made unlikely acquaintances with differing temperaments, characters, and convictions. Further, they came from completely different worlds: Haushofer was an aristocrat, Hitler a vulgar upstart. Haushofer, in fact, was not even a racist: his wife, Martha, was half-Jewish by birth.

Some historians do attribute certain parts of *Mein Kampf* to Haushofer's influence, although this could be either directly or indirectly through Hess. On the other hand, Fest says, with all due credit to outside influences, Hitler's own ideas of geopolitics—that is, expansion of Germany (which became known as *Lebensraum*)—were his own.[22]

Haushofer did play an influential role in the 1936 Anti-Comintern Pact between Germany, Italy, and Japan, and his son, Albrecht, went on several missions to Japan for the Third Riech. But there is little of substance to suggest he had an overpowering influence over Hitler and his decisions.

Perhaps this story throws more light on the truth of Haushofer's so-called influence on Hitler and his role as a guru of the occult, imparter of black magic, etc., than a long, reasoned argument: In 1938 Karl Haushofer was just back from the Convegno Volta African Congress at which colonial problems had been discussed.

Haushofer had asked Hess to arrange a meeting between Hitler and himself. As a result, at the baptism of Hess's son Wolf Rudiger, the two men were left alone together before the fire in Hess's house. Haushofer told Hitler that further territorial demands in Europe would produce great hostility among the Western nations. Instead, Germany should make a deal with Britain guaranteeing national boundaries and promising to waive all right to Poland, provided Britain recognized the status quo and returned German colonies in Africa. Haushofer further suggested that Hitler should visit Britain, as he had received information that certain circles around Chamberlain and Halifax would be willing to listen to such a proposal. The story concludes, "Hitler eyed him stonily as though to say: 'You foolish old man, you have never understood me,' turned on his heel and walked out of the room without a word."[23]

Haushofer was imprisoned for a short time during the war. However, his beliefs were shattered by the destruction of Germany. A final blow was the arrest and execution of his son, Albrecht, for his role in the July 1944 plot against Hitler. On 11 March 1946, Karl and Martha Haushofer set out for a walk in the woods. They stopped about a half kilometer from their house by a stream under a willow tree. There they took poison. Martha was also hanged from the tree.[24]

Had Haushofer carried out his oath as a member of the Green Dragon Society, that is, committed suicide because he had failed in his life's mission? Or was he simply taking the path of many Germans of that time, atoning for the dishonor which had been brought upon their country? Certainly it is hard to attribute Hitler's suicide as a matter of honor, let alone as a result of an oath he swore as part of his initiation many years before in the Green Dragons.

Astrology's Role in Bizarre Affair of Hitler's Deputy

Rudolf Hess believed deeply in astrology and other aspects of the occult,[25] yet his actions led to widespread suffering among astrologers. On 10 May 1941 (an important date in what follows) in a move that provided World War II with one of its greatest and still largely unexplained mysteries, Hess, carrying and wearing, by several accounts, a variety of occult symbols, including a Tibetan amulet,[26] flew alone to Britain and parachuted into a field near Glasgow. He was soon captured and asked to be taken to the Duke of Hamilton. He claimed he was on a mission to enlist British support for Germany in a common attack on Communist Russia. He believed the duke was a politically influential figure.[27]

As soon as he heard what his deputy had done Hitler publicly disowned Hess. Britain, strangely enough, did not treat the capture of the deputy as a propaganda coup or in any other way take advantage of it.[28] It confined itself to a brief official statement that Hess had been captured. Orthodox historian Alan Bullock says the reason for the government's silence was embarrassment and the implication that secret negotiations for a compromise peace might be going on between Britain and Germany.[29] One German was more puzzled than embarrassed: On 16 May, Goebbels recorded in his diary his amazement that the British government "has apparently not hit on the obvious idea of simply issuing statements in Hess's name, without consulting him." This, Goebbels observed, would incense the German people against Hitler. "This is the only—but a dreadful—danger to us," Goebbels wrote. Had he been in charge of British propaganda, he would undoubtedly have made much more of the whole incident.[30]

The above speculation is interesting but does not throw any light on one of the intriguing aspects of the mystery that concerns us: Was the date of the mission randomly selected, or had it been chosen on some astrological or other occult basis? The first indication that astrology or the occult may have been in some way implicated came when German police rounded up those astrologers not currently in jail or in concentration camps and questioned them about what they knew of Hess and the mission.[31]

As we have seen,[32] Hitler's interest in and knowledge of astrology was highly questionable. It appears, however, he was tolerant of Hess's preoccupation with the subject (as indeed he was of Himmler's weakness for the occult[33]), that is, apparently, until the flight of his deputy.

Rudolf Hess was born on 26 April 1894, which makes him, like Hitler, a Taurean. One account has Hess as Hitler's astrologer in secret constantly passing onto Hitler from his various astrology contacts what the stars foretold for Hitler and Germany. Until March 1941 he had consistently predicted good fortune; from then on the stars showed Hitler's meteoric career was approaching its climax.[34]

In Wolf Hess's account of his father's flight, Hitler had discussed the possibility of putting out peace feelers to Britain with Reichs-marshall Hermann Goering, another deputy führer and rival of Hess.[35] It seems that Goering had said to Hitler shortly after the war began, "We must fly to Britain and I'll try to explain the situation," and Hitler, though doubtful, suggested that if he could, he should try it. Goering apparently passed this on to Hess and it lodged in his mind.[36]

Most orthodox accounts say Hitler knew nothing of Hess's mission until a few hours after the latter's Messerschmitt had taken off on 10 May. Hess had left a note and this was delivered to the Führer by courier.

Wolf Hess contends that Hitler did know of his father's plan to fly solo to Britain beforehand and the two men spent time together trying to pinpoint the most auspicious date for it.[37]

Most accounts of Hitler's reaction to the news is that it produced an outburst of fury in which he raged around his study denouncing Hess as a traitor and demanding to know who else was involved.[38] By the time he had finished he had declared Hess to be mentally unbalanced and stripped him of his offices.[39]

On the morning after his capture Hess did meet the young Duke of Hamilton, then an RAF officer. According to official reports, Hess told the duke that this had been his fourth attempt to fly to Scotland. On the other three occasions bad weather had forced him to turn back.[40] (This could be taken as a deliberate attempt by Hess to avoid anyone reading significance into the date on which he did finally succeed. Hess's motives for doing this would have been to prevent ridicule should it become known that there was, as I am hypothesizing, an astrological basis for the choice of the date.)

Hess told the duke that his mission was one of mercy—the Führer was willing to talk peace: it was inevitable Germany would win the war and he wanted to prevent any unnecessary slaughter.[41]

Astrological Advisers

At this stage we must backtrack: Wolf Hess says that his father consulted his old mentor Karl Haushofer late in 1940 and asked him if he thought it was still possible to pursue peace feelers with Britain with any prospect of success.[42] This "evil genius" of the occult obviously failed to invoke any of his powers of prediction to provide an answer to Hess's question. Instead, he referred Hess to his son, Professor Albrecht Haushofer. This was not a decision that ignored the occult altogether for Albrecht was a competent amateur astrologer[43] and professor of political geography at Berlin University. Albrecht also opposed the war with Britain and was involved in the underground opposition to Hitler.

King claims that Albrecht had "an obsessional interest" in Hitler's horoscope[44] and was almost certainly the only one of Hess's occult acquaintances who had both the knowledge of the technical side of astrology to argue for the ending of the war against Britain and the political will to do so in spite of the very real risk of being arrested as a defeatist.[45] (In fact, Albrecht was arrested as soon as Hess's capture had been announced. Although he was later released, he was arrested again, this time for his part in the 20 July 1944 bomb plot against Hitler. For the latter offense, he was executed.)

After some discussions, Albrecht, it seems somewhat reluctantly (because of his pessimism about success), suggested he attempt to arrange a meeting between Hess and the young Duke of Hamilton, "the closest of my British friends," on neutral soil.[46] However, the duke failed to respond to a letter from Albrecht and the anxious months dragged on.[47] Hess had first seen his mentor in September 1940, so Hess's decision to seek peace was neither hasty nor carried out without sufficient thought. In the end, Hess changed his plans. He now wished to meet the duke himself without using Albrecht as an intermediary: if need be, he was prepared to put his own life at risk in the attempt.[48]

Given the importance Hess was by this stage placing on the mission, including the fact that Hitler's stars were showing the Führer was nearing the peak of his destiny—it is impossible to imagine Hess not turning to astrology and other occult sources for signs and portents to help him in his decision to make the flight. In an effort to produce a son and heir, he and his wife had spent six years visiting astrologers, cartomancers, and other workers of magic before they were rewarded with Wolf's birth.[49]

So when it came down to deciding the date Hess, who may not have been "Hitler's astrologer in secret" as the London *Times* speculated, still could not have avoided mentioning to Hitler 10 May 1941, the date on which he took off for Britain, as auspicious both astrologically and coincidentally.

As we have seen, on that day exactly one year before, the astrological position of the stars was shining for Hitler.[50] Hitler had ordered the launch of the offensive that gave most of Western Europe to the Germans. The attack had been opposed as a strategically suitable date by Hitler's generals. Its stunning success was therefore even more of a personal triumph for Hitler.

A member of Hess's staff, Dr. Schulte-Strathaus, had told Hess in January 1941 that an important astronomical event would shortly take place in the constellation of Taurus. This was a conjunction of six planets coinciding with a full Moon. The date of this phenomenon was 10 May 1941.[51] Dr. Schulte-Strathaus, like many academics of that time, was a keen amateur astrologer.

He was also Hess's main adviser on other occult matters. Schulte-Strathaus had been on the staff at the Nazi party headquarters since 1935.[52] The evidence, therefore, begins to mount against 10 May being a date Hess had randomly chosen or one dependent on weather conditions alone.

Searching for other possible reasons why Hess—and possibly Hitler—chose 10 May as a propitious date, I came across a significant coincidence. Krafft, "Hitler's pet astrologer," was born in 1900 on 10 May! Krafft, as a matter of course, would have worked on his progressed horoscope for his forthcoming birthday. In doing so he would have come across the conjunction of the six planets identified by Schulte-Strathaus. He may even have discovered in his own "stars" some further sign of good fortune on that day. In any case, Krafft would almost certainly have done what he did when he correctly predicted the attempt on Hitler's life in 1939[53]—pass the information on to Hess.

My hypothesis is that Hess—and quite possibly Hitler—balanced these various pieces of information and decided that they portended the date on which the mission should go ahead. Naturally, any believer, such as Hess, would see a great deal more significance in these conjunctions than Hitler. Not only should the mission proceed on that day, but it would surely be a success. Hitler, who was partial to omens, even if his attitude toward astrology was scornful, must have been impressed as, indeed, he had been by Krafft's previous accurate prediction of the attempt on his life.

So we have three facts pointing to 10 May: (1) the anniversary of the start of Hitler's most successful war campaign, a day on which astrology had shown the signs could not have been better for him; (2) the conjunction of six planets coinciding with a full Moon; (3) Krafft's birthdate, which I speculate led him to contact Hess once again, albeit partly as a result of wanting to pass on the same information already supplied by Schulte-Strathaus; and of course there was Albrecht's continuous encouragement based on his own astrological expertise.

Hitler was to add one more matter of significance to that date: London's worst blitz of the war. As Hess flew over Scotland,

German bombers flew over London in mass formation and bombed it mercilessly, killing hundreds and damaging major public buildings, including the House of Commons. It was as though the targets had been deliberately selected by Hitler to give the British government a message: Negotiate with Hess. Thirty-three German warplanes failed to return from what was to be the war's last major bomber raid on the British capital, on the night of 10 May! Wolf Hess certainly sees the raid in the terms of reinforcing the message his father carried.[54]

There is a final sum to the equation. The tenth of May 1940, the date that was astrologically so propitious for Hitler, was also one of the most significant dates in the life of his wartime opponent, Winston Churchill. On that day he had replaced the discredited Neville Chamberlain as Prime Minister. Wolf Hess's contention is that Hess was expected when he landed in Scotland—by, among other VIPs, Churchill himself. In other words the mission was not spontaneous but had been carefully planned, which would explain why Hess's plane was not shot down, despite being under hot pursuit as it crossed the coast by fighter planes which were ordered not to fire on it.[55] Among the evidence for preknowledge of the flight, Wolf says that when Churchill's private secretary was informed "somebody had landed," he appeared to know immediately who it was.[56] Was Hess Churchill's anniversary present? Was his mission a joint anniversary present for Hitler and Churchill?

In all this we are left with the question: Could the conjunction of events, anniversaries, and planets be put down to coincidence? Or did they play a role, if only to the extent they influenced Hess in choosing a date? It's a question which may well be tied up in the curious silence that still surrounds this bizarre mission.

There is a final curious aspect to this affair involving the time of day (or rather, night). At 23:07 hours on the night of the tenth, Hess's Messerschmitt disappeared off the British radar screens a few kilometers south of Glasgow: in other words, it crashed. A short time later Hess was on the ground and his mission had officially begun. However, a numerologist points out that in her profession the influence of the following day begins at 11 P.M.

the previous night! Hess had arrived too late, numerologically speaking, to begin his mission!

Rudolf Hess was never released by the allies. He died in Berlin's Spandau prison in 1987. In 1984 his son accused the allied powers of subjecting his father to slow and agonizing death "in order to suppress the historical truth."[57]

And the occult truth?

Notes

1. Gerald Suster, *Hitler: The Occult Messiah* (New York: St. Martin's Press, 1981), pp. 56–57.

2. Ibid., p. 57.

3. Ibid., pp. 56–57.

4. Michael FitzGerald, *Storm Troopers of Satan* (London: Robert Hale, 1990), p. 60.

5. James Douglas-Hamilton, *Motive for a Mission* (London: Macmillan, 1971), p. 19.

6. Suster, *Hitler: The Occult Messiah,* p. 57.

7. Trevor Ravenscroft, *The Spear of Destiny* (York Beach, Me.: Samuel Weiser Inc., 1982), p. 247.

8. Suster, *Hitler,* pp. 57–58.

9. Douglas-Hamilton, *Motive for a Mission,* p. 20.

10. See chapter 14.

11. Suster, *Hitler,* p. 58.

12. Edmund Walsh, *Total Power,* quoted in Douglas-Hamilton, *Motive for a Mission,* p. 20.

13. Ibid., p. 21.

14. Ibid.

15. Ibid., p. 22.

16. Suster, *Hitler: The Occult Messiah,* p. 116.

17. Ibid.

18. See chapter 15 for the story of the affair between Hitler and his niece.

19. Joachim C. Fest, *Hitler* (Hammondsworth, Middlesex, U.K.: Pelican Books, 1977), p. 379.

20. Ravenscroft, *The Spear of Destiny,* pp. 230–34.

21. Douglas-Hamilton, *Motive for a Mission,* p. 22.

22. Fest, *Hitler,* p. 324.

23. Peter Paret, Bulletin of the Institute of Historical Research, quoted in Douglas-Hamilton, *Motive for a Mission,* p. 89.

24. Douglas-Hamilton, *Motive for a Mission,* p. 274–75.

25. Francis King, *Satan and Swastika* (St. Albans, Herts, U.K.: Mayflower Books, 1976), p. 149.

26. Douglas-Hamilton, *Motive for a Mission,* p. 168.

27. Ibid., p. 172.

28. Alan Bullock, *Hitler and Stalin: Parallel Lives* (London: HarperCollins, 1991), p. 788.

29. Ibid.

30. Wolf Rudiger Hess, *My Father, Rudolf Hess* (London: W. H. Allen, 1986), pp. 94–95.

31. Douglas-Hamilton, *Motive for a Mission,* pp. 218–19.

32. See chapter 17.

33. See chapter 11.

34. *London Times,* 14 May 1941, quoted in Ellic Howe, *Urania's Children* (London: William Kimber, 1967), p. 192.

35. Hess, *My Father, Rudolf Hess,* p. 58.

36. Ibid., p. 48.

37. Ibid., p. 68.

38. Bullock, *Hitler and Stalin,* p. 788.

39. Ibid.

40. Douglas-Hamilton, *Motive for a Mission,* p. 40.

41. Ibid., p. 175.

42. Hess, *My Father, Rudolf Hess,* p. 54.

43. King, *Satan and Swastika,* p. 231.

44. Ibid., p. 231.

45. Ibid.

46. Hess, *My Father, Rudolf Hess,* pp. 56–57.

47. Ibid.

48. Ibid., pp. 57–58.

49. King, *Satan and Swastika,* p. 149.

50. See chapter 18.

51. King, *Satan and Swastika,* p. 231.

52. Ibid., p. 231.

53. See chapter 18.

54. Hess, *My Father, Rudolf Hess,* p. 68.

55. Ibid., p. 153.
56. Ibid., p. 155.
57. Ibid., p. 13.

21

Final Cosmic Predictions

Stories of the astrological influence on Hitler and the Nazis survived until the last hours of the Third Reich.

In the final months of the war Walter Schellenberg, the young SS-Brigade führer who was head of Himmler's Foreign Intelligence Department, is reported to have introduced Himmler to astrologer Wilhelm Wulff, who, said Schellenberg, had predicted the attempt on Hitler's life of 20 July 1944.[1]

Wulff, the son of a middle-class Hamburg family, first came into contact with the infant Nazi party and other right-wing organizations in 1923 through an old army friend, Herbert Volck, who attempted to convert his friend to National Socialism, but the astrologer cast the horoscopes for the Nazi leaders and told his friend that his stars were "catastrophically opposed" to those of Hitler, whom he said was likely to "issue cruel and senseless orders and be feared."[2]

Wulff was arrested, like Krafft and so many other astrologers at the time of Hess's erratic flight to Britain, in June 1941. He was released four months later. During the intervening months, he was put to work drawing astrological charts for the SS.[3] At the meeting with Himmler, Wulff predicted a "mysterious death" of the Führer before 7 May 1945. Himmler was so impressed by Wulff that during the last months of the war he "seldom took any steps without first consulting his horoscope."[4]

Schellenberg had been working for nearly a year on a plan to remove Hitler by force from Berlin and hold him, as a nominal but impotent head of state, while Himmler carried on the government. Himmler, with Wulff's approval, had contacted the Swedish diplomat Count Bernadotte on 23 April 1945 and said he was willing to capitulate on the Western front in order to save as much of Germany as possible from the Russians.[5]

When on 29 April, Hitler learned of the contact between the two men, he raged like a maniac, his face turning purple. He ordered Himmler be arrested as a traitor.[6] That same day a despondent Himmler repeatedly asked Wulff what he should do.[7] Wulff suggested he should continue the negotiations or go into hiding. Himmler, whether as a result of Wulff's advice is not known, shaved off his moustache, donned an eyepatch, and fled the scene. Despite this he was recognized by British troops and arrested. On 23 May 1945 he followed Hitler's example and committed suicide by taking a cyanide tablet.[8] Wulff survived the war and his less than willing association with the chief of the Nazi police to write his biography.[9] Wulff does not rate a mention with the orthodox historians such as Bullock, Padfield, and Fest, although a similarly named Karl Wolff does. Wolff did take part in the peace negotiations in the dying stages of the war. He was also a World War I veteran and had, like Hitler, won the Iron Cross First and Second Class. Following the war, he had built a successful career in advertising having created his own agency. When his business became a victim of the economic crash in the early thirties, he signed on with the SS and quickly attracted the attention of Himmler. Padfield says Wolff represented the other face of the SS, reassuringly reasonable, intelligent, realistic, socially ultra-acceptable. He also conformed to the Aryan ideal, six feet tall with blond hair and blue eyes and with a high enough forehead to give his face the required length.[10]

As the war drew to a close Wolff had a number of meetings with Allen Dulles of the Offices of Special Services (OSS) in a safe house in Zurich, claiming he came entirely on his own initiative without the knowledge of Hitler or Himmler. However, Padfield says the circumstantial evidence would indicate he had permission from both men to explore contacts with the West.[11] Wolff does not appear to have been involved in the negotiations between Himmler and Bernadotte. There were in fact parallel negotiations going on. It is obvious that Wulff and Wolff both existed and both worked for Himmler. Howe notes that when he spoke to Wulff in 1962 the astrologer made it clear that he by no means welcomed his personal involvement with Himmler.[12] In the postwar period, Wolff repeated his statement to Dulles "when self-preservation demanded that he keep his American friends and protectors believing he had been acting on his own from the start."[13] The point being made here is that what Padfield calls a "fog of disinformation" was put up then and since concerning Wolff and that confusion may have resulted in attributing a part of his role in the negotiations to the other "wolf," Wilhelm, whether by accident or design. If the latter, it could have been with the aim of reinforcing the supposed influence of astrology and the occult in those final days.

Having examined the role of an astrologer who was supposedly in Himmler's presence and influencing him in peace talks, we cannot ignore another alleged mystic who orthodox history accepts was involved in negotiations between Bernadotte and Himmler, even though his extracurricular powers are not mentioned. This man was Felix Kersten. Generally described simply as Hitler's Finnish masseur, Kersten wrote after the war that he had studied under an Oriental occultist and masseur named Ko in Berlin in the thirties. Ko was involved with Tibetan white magic. Over a period of months he taught Kersten many techniques not only of manipulation but meditation. As a result, when he laid his hands on a patient a flow of energy came from his fingertips and into the body of the patient. He was such a success treating Himmler, who suffered from perennial stomach cramps, that the SS leader begged him to become his personal masseur.[14] In the final years of the war Kersten and Wulff worked tirelessly to persuade Himmler to overthrow Hitler and make peace with the West.[15] As part of this campaign Kersten persuaded Wulff to draw up horoscopes to back their arguments, including one which would show that if Himmler released the Jews, the World Jewish Congress would make representations on his behalf to the British and Americans. Kersten actually brought Zionist representatives to meet Himmler who in the end agreed to their demands, issuing immediate orders to stop the killing of concentration camp prisoners.[16] The white magic he had learned from Ko had caused the change of heart on Himmler's part because it countered Hitler's satanic influence on him, says Kersten.[17]

Secret Report

A secret report compiled by the OSS in 1943 shows that the Allies, or at least the Americans, finally managed to place Hitler and astrology in perspective.[18] That they even had to investigate whether there was a connection shows just how powerful was the belief in such a link.

Noting that "almost all writers have attributed Hitler's confidence to the fact he is a great believer in astrology and that he is constantly in touch with astrologers who advise him concerning his course of action," the report finds that this is almost certainly untrue.[19]

The report by OSS officer Walter Langer, a psychologist, was eventually published in 1972. It concludes:

All of our informants (who they are the report does not say) who have known Hitler rather intimately discard the idea (of Hitler's belief) as absurd. They all agree that nothing is more foreign to Hitler's personality than to seek help from outside sources of this type.[20]

The Führer had never had his horoscope cast [though, as we have seen with Ebertin, many were cast without his asking[21]], but in an indicative move Hitler, some time before the war, forbade the practice of fortune-telling and star-reading in Germany.[22]

The report's findings are unequivocal and show both clear thinking and good security sources. The egregious Louis de Wohl[23] is not mentioned in it, which could be taken as some indication that American security services knew that he had been working as a British secret service operative on his tour of the United States (just before the report would have been compiled) and had gone along with the deception being played on their fellow country-persons, knowing that he could not, in fact, provide them with any insights into Hitler's mind.

The report does speculate on one interesting person we have not so far mentioned. It says Hitler may have been influenced in some ways by an astrologer and "fortune teller" named Hanussen (Eric) in the 1920s. Hanussen, who is elsewhere[24] described as a professional clairvoyant, was, according to Langer,[25] "an extremely clever individual" who taught Hitler a great deal concerning the importance of staging meetings to obtain the greatest dramatic effect.

Hanussen was not interested in the Nazi movement, but through Hitler may have come in contact with a group of astrologers who were very active in Munich at the time and spoke of "another Charlemagne and a new Reich" being portended in the stars.[26]

Hanussen turned up on a Nazi list as one of those murdered by Nazi storm troops in the reign of terror let loose following the Reichstag fire of 27 February 1933.[27] Hitler may have been directly responsible for his mentor's death, as some writers have claimed, citing it as an example of the lengths he was willing to go to disguise his past, including the fact that he was indebted to mystics or occultists. On the other hand, as Fest suggests, his death could have been a bureaucratic oversight, one of the many hundreds of people senselessly killed in that reign of terror.[28] Motives were often tangled in those days.

The Czarina Is Dead

The tendency to seek signs and portents outside reality became frantic among the Nazi leaders as the end came closer.

> In the early part of April (1945) . . . Goebbels sought predictions in . . . horoscopes and while American troops had already reached the foothills of the Alps, while Schleswig-Holstein was cut off and Vienna lost, out of planetary conjunctions, ascendants and transits in the quadrant, hopes once more flickered up of a great turning point in the second half of April.[29]

By coincidence, in this period Goebbels told Count Lutz Schwerin von Krosigk, the Nazi minister for finance, that he had read to Hitler from Carlyle's *History of Frederick the Great* (Hitler's favorite book).[30] The extract details the desperate situation faced by the German king (on whom Hitler believed he modelled himself) in the winter of 1761–62, the darkest period of the Seven Years' War against Russia. All of Frederick's generals and ministers were convinced that he was finished; the enemy already looked upon Prussia as destroyed; the future appeared entirely dark. In a letter to one minister, Count d'Aregenson, Frederick gave himself a final time limit: if there was no change in the situation by 15 February he would give up and take poison. Then, on 5 February, the sign! The Czarina died! Peter III who succeeded her to the throne immediately sued for peace. Goebbels said the words had brought tears to Hitler's war-weary eyes.

All they now needed, he told von Krosigk, was a sign of their own. He went on to say that in the course of a conversation following that reading, he had sent for two horoscopes that were carefully kept in one of Himmler's research departments. One was the horoscope for the Führer, drawn up on 30 January 1933, the other was the horoscope for the Wiemar Republic, dated 9 November 1918. Goebbels found that both horoscopes predicted the outbreak of war in 1939, the victories of 1941, and then the series of defeats culminating in the worst disasters in the early months of 1945, especially in the first half of April. Then there was to be an overwhelming victory in the second half of April, stagnation until August, and, in August, peace. After the peace there would be a difficult time for Germany for three years; but from 1948 she would rise to greatness again.[31]

King dismisses suggestions that the horoscopes may have been fake creations of Himmler's research department, or that they were drawn up with the advantage of hindsight.[32]

Late at night on 12 April, after a heavy air raid on Berlin, von Krosigk and some cronies were drinking when the phone rang. "The state-secretary wished to speak to me," von Krosigk wrote. "What could he want at so late an hour. He only uttered one short sentence: Roosevelt is dead."[33] The Sign!

At the news of the death of the American president, "we felt the wings of the Angel of History rustle through the room. Could this be the long desired change of fortune?" Next morning he telephoned Goebbels to put to him that this was indeed the portent for which they had all been waiting.

Goebbels had already heard the news. He told von Krosigk that the previous evening he had stayed at General Busse's head-quarters at Kuestrin (on the Eastern front) and later, sitting with the officers, had developed a thesis that a portent such as had happened to Frederick the Great was needed for reasons of "historical necessity and justice." One of the officers had skeptically and ironically asked: "What czarina will die this time?"

After driving home, where he heard the news, he had put a late call through to Busse and said, "The czarina is dead!" Goebbels had called for champagne, then made another late-night call to Hitler. "My Führer, I congratulate you!" he shouted into the telephone. "Roosevelt is dead. It is written in the stars that the second half of April will be the turning point for us. Today is Friday 13 April. It is the turning-point."[34]

Some writers say Hitler did take the coincidence of the czarina's and president's deaths as corroboration that Providence had given him a final miraculous intervention. But any exhilaration generated as a result soon evaporated.

Naturally, Roosevelt's death did not affect the outcome of

the war and within days Hitler had done what Frederick had been saved from doing two hundred years before—he committed suicide by taking poison, as did Goebbels.

Notes

1. Francis King, *Satan and Swastika* (St. Albans, Herts, U.K.: Mayflower Books, 1976), p. 242.

2. Ibid., pp. 242–43.

3. Ibid., p. 243.

4. H. R. Trevor-Roper, *The Last Days of Hitler,* 4th ed. (London: Macmillan, 1971), pp. 95–97.

5. King, *Satan and Swastika,* p. 247.

6. Joachim C. Fest, *Hitler* (Hammondsworth, Middlesex, U.K.: Pelican Books, 1977), p. 1106.

7. King, *Satan and Swastika,* p. 257.

8. Ibid., p. 252.

9. Ellic Howe, *Urania's Children* (London: William Kimber, 1967), p. 239.

10. Peter Padfield, *Himmler Reichsführer-SS* (New York: Henry Holt and Company, 1990), p. 136.

11. Ibid., p. 573.

12. Ibid., p. 239.

13. Ibid., p. 576.

14. Felix Kersten, *The Kersten Memoirs,* cited in Michael FitzGerald, *Storm Troopers of Satan* (London: Robert Hale, 1990), pp. 169–70.

15. FitzGerald, *Storm Troopers of Satan,* p. 168.

16. Brennan, *The Occult Reich,* cited in FitzGerald, *Storm Troopers of Satan,* pp. 170–71.

17. Kersten, *The Kersten Memoirs,* cited in FitzGerald, *Storm Troopers of Satan,* p. 171.

18. Walter Langer, *The Mind of Adolf Hitler* (New York: Basic Books, 1972), pp. 31–32.

19. Ibid., p. 31.

20. Ibid., p. 32.

21. See chapter 17.

22. Langer, *The Mind of Adolf Hitler,* p. 32.

23. See chapter 18.
24. Fest, *Hitler,* p. 596.
25. Langer, *The Mind of Adolf Hitler,* p. 32.
26. Ibid.
27. Fest, *Hitler,* p. 596.
28. Ibid.
29. Ibid., p. 1090.
30. Trevor-Roper, *The Last Days of Hitler,* pp. 109–13.
31. Ibid.
32. King, *Satan and Swastika,* p. 276.
33. Trevor-Roper, *The Last Days of Hitler,* pp. 109–13.
34. Ibid.

22

Conclusions

When it comes to occult practice we have more evidence to show the involvement of his greatest wartime foe, the British prime minister, Winston Churchill! Churchill belonged to an organization steeped in occultism and, on joining, took a barbaric oath in which he accepted having his throat cut and his tongue torn out should he divulge its secrets.[1] Churchill was a member of the British Parliament when he stepped into the magic world of occultism in 1903 by being initiated into the Order of Freemasons.[2]

We cannot in all honesty say the same thing about Hitler. Even the occult historian King doubts the claims that Hitler was a member of the one secret society of any influence he is most likely to have joined, the Thule Society. As for the group's "monstrous, sadistic, magic initiation ritual," which Ravenscroft claims Hitler underwent, King says, as we have seen, no such ceremony ever took place.

In public Hitler made a specific denunciation of Freemasons and other secret societies and their activities in a speech to the Reich Party Congress of 1938. We have seen other positive evidence for his anti-occultism: He persecuted occult groups and individuals, including the Thule Society, with its strong links to the precursor of the Nazis, the Worker's party.

Furthermore, it was not in Hitler's character to be a "joiner." The weight he gives in *Mein Kampf* to his anguishing over his

231

decision to join the one organization he did commit himself to—
the Worker's party, which became the National Socialists—is
evidence of that. He was an avid follower of politics in his early
Vienna days, but did not join a party. His character, temperament,
ego, and undisciplined mind were all factors mitigating against
him becoming a member of any body to whom he would have
had to subordinate himself. It would have been out of character
for him to adopt or be influenced by any substantial body of
arcane and/or magical beliefs for any sustained length of time.

We are told and must accept with some credibility that Hitler
was unimpressed by Himmler's attempts to turn the SS into a
quasi-occult body, and evidence has not been produced to show
Hitler ever visited the SS palace at Wewelsberg where its members
performed their alleged "magic" rituals.

Americans are reminded daily of the occult influences on their
country through the symbols on the dollar bill: the Great Seal
of the United States with its pyramid with the eye above it is
an obvious reference to freemasonry (the unfinished pyramid represents the Temple of Solomon; the eye represents the Mason's
god known as the Grand Architect of the Universe).[3] Other symbols
such as the thirty-two feathers of the eagle on the seal are also
seen as masonic symbols and the thirteen stars above the eagle's
head form a Star of David (King David is an essential part of
Freemasonry legend).[4]

Among the American presidents who swore Freemasonry's
bloody oaths and took part in its occult rituals were: Washington,
Monroe, Jackson, Polk, Buchanan, Andrew Johnson, Garfield,
McKinley, both Franklin and Teddy Roosevelt, Taft, Harding,
Truman, and Ford.

On the other hand, in Nazi Germany we had the symbolic
ambiguity of the swastika as discussed in chapter 12.

Any secret society, no matter how benevolent its face, creates
a feeling of some unease within the wider community in which
it operates, whether in Nazi Germany or the Western democracies.
If it sets out to have an influence on that wider society, then it
cannot stay an entirely secret body for long, the point being that

it is not tenable to argue that Hitler belonged to some secret organization whose name, aims, and philosophy remain a mystery to this day, except to certain occultists.

From early in their rise to power Hitler and his Nazis were enveloped in an aura of mysticism almost despite themselves. This aura *appears* closer to the experience of occultism than any other major movement in the twentieth century. Hitler came to personify the invisible structure which became the occult myth dealt with here.

With the help of contemporary occult writers, the illusion is today more pervasive. We find no such occult mystique surrounding other aberrations of civilization, as represented by Stalin, Pol Pot, Saddam Hussein, or the like.

There is even a source: the folklore of German history, with its legends of a Master Race, Aryan Supermen. Here is where Hitler and his followers drew their inspiration! Those are the images they invoked! As a result of all this, writers such as Ravenscroft have been able to depart so far from historical fact as to construct a synthetic—an *ersatz*—history of Hitler and claim it as the truth. Ravenscroft's fanciful material, which we have considered in some detail in all its contradictions and untenable claims, is not alone. Other writers, such as FitzGerald, reinforce the myth as truth. Another of the occult historians, Howard, has Hitler proclaiming (as evidence) in 1934, "We shall form an Order, the Brotherhood of the Templars around the Holy Grail of the pure blood."[5] However, Suster, dealing with the same material, has Hitler *suggesting*: ". . . shall we form an Order . . . ?"[6] The transposition of just two words changes the tenor of Hitler's supposed attitude to the idea of occult orders from positive and eager to tentative and doubtful. It is these contradictions that alert us to cracks in the myth.

Based on the material analyzed in the preceding chapters, we are able to reject claims that Hitler had supernatural powers of his own or that he weighed his every move based upon whether this or that omen was favorable—intriguing omens there were, as we have seen, but who was there in the end to bring a bad omen to his attention?

Hitler was quite simply an opportunist who would and did use whatever was in his grasp, including the occult, if it would further his agenda, without affording such ideas, beliefs, systems, trends, or ideologies either respect or acknowledgment. Once their use had passed they would be quickly dropped and quite possibly banned and their adherents persecuted.

His parents demonstrated no psychic abilities or delved in the occult other than their normal religious obligations. In young Adolf's case, the unique set of circumstances that go to forming a personality included clinical afflictions, an overbearing father, and the climate of the times together with that ineffable dose of chance circumstance to be found in all human affairs.

In his youth and early adulthood Hitler's irresponsible, unguided, and malformed personality was open to all sorts of wild suggestions and half-baked ideas, so long as they did not involve work. The few deep-seated convictions he was to adopt—his virulent nationalism and anti-Semitism—were to stick with him "granite-like" and irrationally for the rest of his life. The occult influences he is said to have been open to at this time are unproven.

From early in his life Hitler claimed to be led by an inner voice, the voice, it appears, of Providence. "I go with the assurance of a sleepwalker on the way Providence dictates," he told a party rally in Munich on 15 March 1936. This longstanding relationship with "Providence" is cited as further evidence of his being in touch with the supernatural. But it can only be positively seen as evidence of his acceptance of a Higher Order, despite his *hubris*. He had the sense not to agree with plans of other Nazi leaders to replace Christianity with their "religion" by making *Mein Kampf* a Bible and substituting in churches the swastika for the cross.

Hitler's abilities as an orator at Nazi rallies and in his broadcasts is presented as further evidence of his communing with some supernatural forces. But we see the same effect on an almost daily basis at rock concerts and religious rallies. Incidentally, today's rock stars are, like Hitler, accused of involvement in the occult, devil worship, and sexual excesses to a disproportionate extent.

Whatever went on with Hitler's sex life in private (see chapter

15), his public performances did have all the overt erotic arousal of a modern-day pop concert. The crowd at first holding its collective breath being worked into a state of increasing excitement of release: building to a climax that comes with a rush: a final release of ecstasy.[7] Other contemporary observers have tried to describe the sensually charged rallies as inspired by the devil.

In fact, Hitler was the first of history's mass media figures. No political leader had before him used rallies, broadcasts, and film for propaganda purposes. Ironically, unlike today's media figures, he managed to keep the facts about his private life hidden, even though sexuality was an intrinsic part of his public appearances.

Conversely he generated the same kind of hypnotic emotions as a modern-day preacher stirring a religious crusade: "I . . . do not know how to describe the emotions that swept over me as I heard this man. His words were like a scourge . . . the gospel he preached a sacred truth. He seemed another Luther. I forgot everything but the man; then glancing round I saw that his magnetism was holding thousands as one . . . the intense will of the man, the passion of his sincerity seemed to flow from him and into me. I experienced an exaltation that could be likened only to religious conversion," wrote Kurt Luedecke, author of *I Knew Hitler,* in 1938.[8]

What of the uniformed Nazi masses who played such an obvious symbolic role at these rallies? They were explained away as harmless in 1933 by America's ambassador to Poland, the Wisconsin millionaire John Cudahy. He visited Germany on his way to his post in Poland and while noting in a report to Roosevelt that the allegiance to Hitler borders on fanaticism, he went on to say as for the Brownshirts, the Blackshirts (who were at that time assaulting Jews in the streets), and the Hitler Youth they were simply an outlet "for the peculiar social need of a country which loves display and pageantry. Half the Brownshirts are unemployed and the organization provides relief and cheap meals for needy members. These marching clubs are essentially social. The German feels important and distinguished in a uniform and what has been taken as a blatant display of militarism is merely an expression of the unique German gregarious instinct, accountable on the same grounds that our Elks . . . are accountable." Roosevelt had trouble accepting the analogy.[9]

As the final chapters show, astrology played an intriguing part in Hitler's life. Germany was in the grip of an "astrology fever" as Hitler clawed his way to power. What is surprising is that he was able to be so objective about a subject that was such a sinecure for so many of his countrypersons. It can be seen as an example of his opportunistic streak: once he saw that astrology could no longer serve him—and the flight of Hess must finally have disillusioned him—then he rejected it and persecuted its followers.

Unfortunately, when we look for personal records to prove or disprove a thesis in relation to Hitler, we have only the turgid prose of his appalling *Mein Kampf*. There are no letters, diaries, or notes that would give an inkling to his inner thought processes at any stage, or serve future generations of researchers. He was as meticulous as a spy in the field, leaving no clues, nothing to link him to another human being, influence, or legacy of achievement. Nothing he created survived him, no monuments. He did not even leave that most mercenary of human relics, a bank account! It was, indeed, as though he had come and gone by magic.

Fifty years since his death and he remains an enigma! However, allowing false and fanciful claims about Hitler to go unchallenged will not help us unwrap that enigma. This book is a small effort to correct some of those claims.

Notes

1. Stephen Knight, *The Brotherhood* (London: Panther, 1983), p. 317.

2. Ibid., p. 36.

3. William Poundstone, *Big Secrets* (London: Corgi Books, 1985), p. 77.

4. Ibid., p. 78.

5. Michael Howard, *The Occult Conspiracy* (London: Rider, 1989), p. 131.

6. Gerald Suster, *Hitler: The Occult Messiah* (New York: St. Martin's Press, 1981), p. 49.

7. Joachim C. Fest, *Hitler* (Hammondsworth, Middlesex, U.K.: Pelican Books, 1977), p. 481.

8. Ibid., p. 230.

9. Ted Morgan, *FDR* (New York: Simon and Schuster, 1985), pp. 395–96.

Index